The Bridge Builder Method

Bob,
Thanks you for so many years of friendship and inspiration!

John

The Bridge Builder Method

The exact secrets used by top influencers and digital marketers to quickly build multi-million dollar companies.

By Joshua T Boswell

The Bridge Builder Method is a work of nonfiction. Some names and identifying details have been changed.

Copyright © 2022 by Joshua T Boswell

All rights reserved. No part of this book may be reproduced by any mechanical, photographic, or electronic process, other than for "fair use" as brief quotations embodied in articles and reviews, without prior written permission of the publisher.

This book is intended for educational purposes only and does not constitute business or legal advice. Nor is this intended to replace the advice of professional consultants and advisors. These is no guarantee of success or promise of specific outcomes or income. Neither the author or the publisher assumes liability for any losses or gains that may arise from the use of the strategies and principles in this book. All such liabilities are expressly disclaimed herewith. In the event you use any of the information in this book for yourself or any of your clients. the author and the publisher assume no responsibility for your actions.

Published in the United States of America by Books to Hook Publishing, LLC.

Paperback ISBN 978-1-959039-53-2
Ebook ISBN 978-1-959030-54-9
Audiobook ISBN 978-1-959-39-55-6

First Edition

www.strahes.com

The Bridge Builder

An old man going a lone highway,
Came, at the evening cold and gray,
To a chasm vast and deep and wide.
Through which was flowing a sullen tide
The old man crossed in the twilight dim,
The sullen stream had no fear for him;
But he turned when safe on the other side
And built a bridge to span the tide.

"Old man," said a fellow pilgrim near,
"You are wasting your strength with building here;
Your journey will end with the ending day,
You never again will pass this way;
You've crossed the chasm, deep and wide,
Why build this bridge at evening tide?"

The builder lifted his old gray head;
"Good friend, in the path I have come," he said,
"There followed after me to-day
A youth whose feet must pass this way.
This chasm that has been as naught to me
To that fair-haired youth may a pitfall be;
He, too, must cross in the twilight dim;
Good friend, I am building this bridge for him!"
~ *by Will Allen Dromgoole*

Entrepreneurs are the dreamers and creators of all advances and improvements for mankind. They are the bridge builders, going before their fellow humans, risking the unknown to open new worlds for those that follow safely afterwards.

**This book is dedicated to you,
the Bridge Builders of the world.**

CONTENTS

Introduction:	The Could vs Should Curse...............	1
Chapter 1:	The Secret Box Top...........................	9
Chapter 2:	Tools Only Used By Professionals.........	26
	Phase One: Meet.........................	**35**
Chapter 3:	How to Grab and Hold Attention...........	39
Chapter 4:	Paid Ads Secrets That Pay...................	73
	Phase Two: Friend........................	**100**
Chapter 5:	How to Get People to Buy - Now!.........	103
Chapter 6:	The Secret to Triple Revenues..............	137
Chapter 7:	Convert Small Buyers to Big Buyers......	151
Chapter 8:	Turn "Thank You" Into Income.............	166
	Phase Three: Bestie.....................	**180**
Chapter 9:	The Hands-Free Wealth Formula...........	184
Conclusion:	The "Bridge" That Saved a Life.............	206

INTRODUCTION

The Could vs Should Curse

In 2005, I attended a five-day marketing seminar in Miami, FL. I walked in with a feeling of intense focus and utter terror. As I sat down, I had to forcefully tighten my quads to keep my legs from shaking.

"Margie," I said to my wife before I left our home in Helena, MT. "I am going to win this time. I just feel it. This business will finally be the one for us. I know your dad is frustrated with me and wants the $5,000 back that we borrowed from him. And I know we still owe $200,000 to the past investors, but I'm determined to pay them back, plus make a great life for us."

"I know you will. I've always believed in you. You just need the right plan. Maybe this one will be it," she said.

I had just started a new business and needed clients to feed our six children. And to get clients, I needed a marketing plan. Not a bunch of ideas… a real step-by-step plan that I could follow and get results from.

To be honest, the seminar was amazing!

For five days, I listened to more than a dozen speakers share their very best ideas on what I COULD do to launch, grow, and profit from my new business.

At least once a day, a surprise gift would be placed on my chair during a break. Usually, it was a book or guide telling me even more things I COULD do to make money.

At the end of the five days, I was utterly exhausted… and mind-bogglingly confused.

I went home and reviewed more than 100 pages of notes.

"Ok," I thought, "this is all the stuff I COULD do… but I'm still totally confused about what I SHOULD do right now to make money."

I didn't have a game plan.

No playbook.

No step-by-step instructions.

Just a massive amount of information on all the things that COULD be done.

In some ways, I felt worse off than I did before the event. I certainly was no closer to making money.

In fact, I felt like I was further away because now, instead of getting to work on a specific plan, I had to spend days sorting through all this info. And use a ton of my energy to make decisions about what I was actually going to do.

And, maybe the most dreadful thing was the feeling of uncertainty.

With so many options to choose from, what was the best option for me right now? And what if I picked the wrong path and wasted my time and money?

That struck fear and dread into my heart.

My family simply could not afford that. We were already eating oatmeal two times a day, supplemented with popcorn and potatoes.

I wanted a simple, clear road that I could drive down with great confidence, knowing that every inch of the path was actually useful... every move was putting me closer to my goal of getting rich.

After a great deal of wasted time trying to figure it all out, I finally picked a path... and sure enough, it was useless. I wasted the last bit of money I had to invest in my business, and got zero results.

In desperation, I picked another marketing road. Maybe out of sheer luck or tenacity or a gift from God, I was able to make that system work. It took me nine months and untold hours, but I made it work.

All of that heartache and wasted time and money could have easily been avoided if an experienced marketer would have put their arm around me and given me a proven, simple playbook.

Today, I'm offering to be your coach. I'm putting my arm around you, looking you in the eyes, and saying:

"This will work. Just do this and you'll get results. No, it is not the only way—there are lots of ways to make this work. But don't worry about all that other stuff. Just focus with me on the simple steps I'll show you. Build each step, one at a time. Each step is proven and rapidly gets you closer to your goal of making money and making a difference."

This book is not about what you COULD do... it is a detailed playbook with a specific plan. It shows you what you SHOULD do right now to make money and get your masterpiece into the world.

If you're ready to do that, let's begin...

Is This Book for You?

This is a playbook for serious entrepreneurs - the Bridge Builders of the world.

A step-by-step guide.

I give you specific instructions about what you should do right now to create an engine that will generate sales in the next 30-90 days, depending on how fast you work the plan.

This book is not a comprehensive encyclopedia on digital marketing. It's not a list of all the things you could do, and the deep reasons and psychology behind them.

You can find those kinds of insights in our other courses, books, mastermind groups, and private coaching.

I'm not going to fill your head with options and press a million decisions on your mind. In fact, the only real serious decisions you'll make are defining your Big Idea and your Compelling Offer. Everything else is a subset of those two decisions.

The instructions on what to do with those decisions is specifically laid out for you in this plan.

This book is about action, clarity, and rapid results.

This book is for you if you:

- Have a solution to a known problem and can deliver that solution in a course, software, book, or other digital format.
- Want to make money within the next 30-90 days by selling your solution online.
- Are curious about the deeper secrets of digital marketing, but right now, you simply want to implement proven tactics that will give you results.
- Are frustrated with mountains and mountains of secrets, strategies, teaching, and books most gurus tell you to consume before you can begin making money. Maybe you've already invested hundreds or thousands of dollars in training information... and still are not sure what to do to get results.

- Have a passion to give value to mankind and a desire to be a Bridge Builder, knowing you will read massive financial and emotional rewards for your efforts.

This book is not for you if you:

- Have an established funnel and marketing system, but want to 10x your income. We can help you do that with our other courses, books, mastermind groups, consulting, and done-for-you services. Please contact us at www.Strahes.com/advanced.
- Have no idea what to offer the world and want help figuring out your value statement and transformational offer. Again, we can help with that, but not here.
- Are obsessed with endless learning but not really concerned with getting results. This book will be much too direct and result-oriented for you.
- Inside this book, you'll get specific instructions. In some cases, I'll need to show you what to do... or you'll need a simple tool or software to make it happen. I created a "Toolbox" for you and provide it as a bonus.

You can access your Toolbox here at www.Strahes.com/builder-tools

What Others Say About Joshua's Systems

"Joshua is a creative talent who understands marketing. His strategies are always excellent and come with lots of "pulling power." I use him often and will continue to work with him in the future. Thanks Joshua!"
~ **Gary Chappell, Nightingale-Conant, CEO**

"Joshua is an amazing marketing teacher! Tough enough to have high standards for his students, but extremely approachable, encouraging, and helpful as well. Just the right balance of everything. I learned far more from him in one month than I learned in an entire semester in college. And unlike many college classes (business or otherwise), every piece of information is straightforward, logical, and actionable in real life. Thanks, Joshua!"
~ **Lynn Churchill, Digital Marketer**

"Joshua provides a comprehensive understanding of sales processes, web traffic, market research and customer psychology. A top pick."
~ **Perry Marshall, Perry Marshall & Associates, Owner, Author of "The Definitive Guide to Google Adwords", "Ultimate Guide to Google Adwords", and "Evolution 2.0"**

"Joshua is gifted.... With his skills, he has converted prospects into lifetime clients or customers."
~ **Dr. Leslie Ademola, Top 100 Influencer in Marketing and Advertising**

"Joshua, thanks for the work you did on the website. I've got to tell you—working with you was not only professionally rewarding... it was fun. I really enjoyed it. During most of this project, we were all in new waters, but you helped us through and made it easy to get finished up. On top of that, the copy was awesome—you nailed the message, the tone and the content. Thanks again for all your hard work."
~ **Kit Schutte, Easter Seals-Goodwill Northern Rocky Mountain, Inc**

"Joshua is someone I highly recommend. Poised, engaging, confident, approachable, funny, knowledgeable, well regarded."
~ **Drew Bischoff, Hybrid Events, CEO**

"Joshua Boswell is an extraordinary trainer. The overarching theme of his life is his love for God, his wife and family.... He's knowledgeable. He's funny. He's irreverent. He's wise. Joshua Boswell is a world-class trainer."
~ **Virginia Farris,** Writer, Author, and Editor

"Joshua is a wealth of knowledge and insight. His calm, no-nonsense approach is refreshing! His mentoring has been invaluable and I can't thank him enough for the personal and business growth he's helped me to achieve. If you are looking for someone who can break down the steps to success into attainable goals…look no further. He is a joy to work with and his desire to help others succeed is apparent in his devotion."
~ **Jennifer Renee, Copywriter and Marketing Consultant**

"I endorse Joshua with gusto! You can tell Joshua practices what he preaches—he's an all-around wonderful person and an asset to any organization."
~ **Laura Rodini, Paisley Green LLC, CEO**

"Joshua is incredibly good at what he does. In my humble opinion by working with Joshua, of course you will get some great ROI but the real value is to feel inspired to become a better person. And this is priceless."
~ **Tevin Gongo, Halifax Consulting**

"If you want the framework or structure to hang your marketing hat on, Joshua Boswell's program is for you. No longer will you stand still with indecision. Instead, you'll get actionable steps you can take to achieve your goals. And, I might add, you'll have fun along the way."
~ **Jewel Pickert, Conflitel Resolutions LLC, Owner**

"As an experienced writer and marketer, I can't believe how much I gained by attending this conference and being Joshuafied! What did I walk away with? Great gems about tricks & techniques, practical steps so we can all bulldoze through our stuck points, excellent templates, a doable and brilliant roadmap and perhaps most important, inspiration on a profound level. I'm truly grateful."
~ Barbara Field, Writing Life Stories, Founder

"Speaking one-on-one with Joshua set me on the right path to achieve my goals. I was floundering with my business and didn't have a clue what to do. Joshua gave me simple to follow step by step instructions to launch my career and my confidence. Thanks for your guidance Joshua it was invaluable."
~ Brett Denton, BS, PICP, IYCA, Kvell Fitness and Nutrition

CHAPTER 1

The Secret Box Top

"Joshua, I know what I have to offer will help a lot of people grieving with the loss of a loved one. I just don't know how to get it out there."

To be honest, I was confused by Irene's comment.

She and I were both in a very expensive mastermind group with one of the top marketers in the world.

Irene invited my wife, Margie, and I to lunch to talk about how she could market her book and podcast. Her story of losing her husband and other family members was incredible. The tools and mindset she'd used to overcome her grief and find a life of extreme joy and happiness were amazing.

Margie and I sat crying with her and marveling at the great gift she had to offer.

"Irene," I said. "I'm not sure I understand. We've just been through several days of training on how to market your idea. What is holding you back?"

Her answer reminded me of where I had been 15 years earlier.

"I know all the things I could do, I'm just not sure where to start and how it all fits together."

Maybe you feel like Irene, where you have something amazing to offer the world but don't know how to get it out there?

Have you been through a thousand courses and programs and still feel confused? It's like someone dumped a 500-piece puzzle on your desk but hid the box top box top. You know all the pieces are there, but don't know what the end picture looks like.

Let me give you the box top box top.

The hard reality is this…

Marketing in today's world is complex. There are a lot of moving parts, and every part needs to operate in harmony with the other parts. Get one thing out of place and the whole system could collapse and cost you a ton of time and money.

I can't change this for you.

But I can help you assemble the pieces in a step-by-step fashion that simplifies the process. We will ensure that you get everything working together the first time to bring in the maximum profits.

I want you to know that I believe in you.

I believe that you are smart enough, strong enough, persistent enough, wise enough, and have enough to offer the world to create a successful business. This book is a testament to my belief in you.

I especially believe that you have something amazing and valuable to offer the world. There is something inside of you that only you have. You have a gift for the rest of us that you—and ONLY you—can provide.

I am here to be your coach and help you create and share that gift.

In very simple terms, you only need to do three things:

1. Define Your Transformational Idea
2. Create a Compelling Offer
3. Build a Funnel to Profitably Sell that Offer

Let me give you the box top so you can see the key pieces of the puzzle and how they fit together.

Define Your Transformational Idea

Every human being has a desire to grow and become better... and we have an imagination to visualize that growth before it happens.

This sets us apart from all the other creatures in the universe.

We want to transform ourselves and our circumstances from where we are right now to something more joyful, more powerful, more peaceful, more prosperous, more impactful.

As an influencer, your role is to fire the imagination and help the rest of us see more clearly what is possible.

You help unlock our minds to see further and believe deeper that the intense longings of the heart are possible. You provide a path for growth, along with the tools and the experience to get there.

As we'll discuss later, you are a Bridge Builder, going before the rest of us, clearing the way and building bridges over the chasms and gaps that separate us from the "more" we seek.

Your Transformational Idea contains both the vision of what is possible for the rest of us and the roadmap for how to get there.

What transformation do you believe we can undergo in our lives? What are the steps for us to achieve that new life?

The answers to these questions represent your Transformational Idea.

Those answers also define the "reason why" your ideal buyer needs to spend money with you.

They will ask themselves, "Why should I spend my hard-earned money on this book, course, program, or event? How will it change my life? How will it help me become a better person? How will it help me resolve the pain points in my life?"

Your Transformational Idea answers those questions for them.

This book presupposes that you have a pretty clear idea of what your Transformational Idea is and can articulate it. Still, we will do some exercises to bring greater clarity and persuasive pulling power to your ideas.

Elon Musk says, "You get paid in direct proportion to the difficulty of problems you solve."

Your offer needs to solve a known problem or fulfill a known desire. That's what makes it compelling.

Create a Compelling Offer

Your Transformational Idea is powerless to effect change without a Compelling Offer.

The Compelling Offer is the delivery system for your Transformational Idea.

Think about it like this...

The Transformational Idea behind the iPhone was that it simplified complex technologies and put them all in our pockets. It has transformed communications, photography, music, productivity, and dozens of other activities in our lives.

What if Steve Jobs had told a few friends that he made a cool gadget and sat them down in his living room and said, "Hey, check out this cool new smartphone. Anyone want one?"

Would the iPhone have taken the world by storm?

Never.

The presentation, the packaging, and the pitch are vital to making your Transformational Idea reach the right audience and persuade them to buy.

In many ways, the format of how you offer your Transformational Idea is almost irrelevant. You can use so many different ways to help your ideal buyer and implement your Idea.

Different formats include:
- Books
- Online Courses—Video, Audio, and Written
- Webinars
- Live Events
- Seminars and Workshops
- Consulting
- Masterminds
- Coaching—Group and Private
- Podcasts
- Communities

We will dig deeper into how you create this compelling offer and package and present your Transformational Idea.

We'll just make sure that you're presenting it in a compelling way and have an audience big enough to meet your goals and aspirations.

A Funnel To Sell It

A "funnel" is a system where you take someone from one level of purchasing from you and move them up to another level.

If they have never heard of you, a funnel system introduces you to them and inspires them to make their first purchase.

If they have already purchased from you, a funnel helps them buy from you again (and again… and again… and again).

You will sell your Compelling Offer through a simple sales funnel.

You don't need a fancy website or mountains of social media content to get started. You need to keep it very simple and focus on making the initial sale.

My friend and mentor, business magnate, Mark Ford, says the first two steps of any business organization are to:

1. Verify the demand for your Transformational Idea
2. Discover your Optimal Selling Strategy (OSS)
3. Verify the Demand

"I've done everything you've told me, Joshua, but I'm still not landing any clients. I think your system is broken," Sue said (not her real name… I changed it for privacy reasons).

I smiled.

"Maybe my system is broken, but let's look at your offer. What are you selling?"

"I want to be a freelance copywriter, writing emails and long-copy sales letters."

"Ok. That's a great industry. Lots of money there. What's your niche? Who are you selling your writing services to?"

"Equestrian nutritional companies. I love horses and know all about them. It will be easy for me to write that stuff. But no one seems to want to buy my services."

I smiled again.

"Well, let's take a look at some of the top companies and see what they are offering."

We pulled up half a dozen websites that sell to both consumers and veterinarians.

It was just as I suspected.

"What kind of copy do you see on their pages?"

"Lots of articles and catalog copy."

"Right," I said. "Do you get a lot of emails from these people? Do they have newsletters? Do you see any long-copy sales letters?"

"No, but that stuff really works well in other industries. I'm sure I can convince them to use it and I know it will help them."

"I know that sounds nice—giving them something that they don't really want or use but that you think they should want and use—but in reality, they don't use emails and long copy because they don't need to. It's not part of their business model or core needs. You need to sell to a known demand."

I have the same advice for you.

Yes, you are here to fire up the imagination and build bridges, but it needs to be done within the scope of a known demand.

Steve Jobs didn't invent the phone, MP3 player, handheld computer, or the internet... he simply created a different way to meet the demands already alive and kicking in those industries.

One of my favorite stories about this topic comes from Russell Conwell's famous speech, "Acres of Diamonds". It is the story about A.T. Steward, the wealthiest retailer in the world in the mid-1800s. Here's what happened, as Conwell shared in his talk...

> "A. T. Stewart, the great princely merchant of New York, the richest man in America in his time, was a poor boy; he had a dollar and a half and went into the mercantile business. But he lost eighty-seven and a half cents of his first dollar and a half because he bought some needles and thread and buttons to sell, which people didn't want.
>
> "He did not know what people needed, and consequently bought something they didn't want, and had the goods left on his hands—a dead loss. A. T. Stewart learned there the great lesson of his mercantile life and said. 'I will never buy anything more until I first learn what the people want; then I'll make the purchase.' He went around to the doors and asked them what

they did want, and when he found out what they wanted, he invested his sixty-two and a half cents and began to supply a 'known demand.' I care not what your profession or occupation in life may be; I care not whether you are a lawyer, doctor, housekeeper, teacher or whatever else, the principle is precisely the same. We must know what the world needs first and then invest ourselves to supply that need, and success is almost certain.

"A. T. Stewart went on until he was worth forty million." (Acres of Diamonds, Russell Conwell)

Make sure your Transformational Idea has a "known demand".

If your idea solves a known problem or fulfills a known desire, then it will sell. People will always buy something that is important to them... something that relieves pain and/or brings joy.

Optimal Selling Strategy (OSS)

Your Optimal Selling Strategy is the combination of benefits, messaging, advertising, packaging, and persuasion points that move people to spend their money with you.

It is the words and images that get people to trust you and believe that your Compelling Offer can and will transform their lives... moving them from where they are to a higher state.

I have good news for you...

Because your offer is something that can be delivered digitally, the OSS you will use is a sales funnel.

This book is dedicated to helping you put the pieces of that OSS puzzle together so you can consistently and repeatedly persuade your ideal buyer to do business with you.

Here is what your funnel will look like. I'll outline it in the order that your ideal buyer will experience it.

You'll also use this outline as a blueprint to actually build the funnel:

The Bridge Funnel

Phase 1: Meet

- Paid Ads → Free Offer (Name, Email)

Phase 2: Friend

- Low Cost Offer (Buy Now) + In Cart Bump Offer → One-Time Offer (Buy Now) → Thank You Page and Surprise Offer
- One Transaction
- Follow Up Sequence

Phase 3: Bestie

- Fulfillment Sequences
- Nurturing Sequence

1 – Paid Ads

Yes, you need to run some paid ads. You don't need a huge budget. In most cases, you can spend as little as $5 or $10 per day and get great results.

I built a list of about 5,000 buyers (not free opt-in list people... buyers) over a six-month period of time with a daily ad spend budget of $10-$15, or less than $2,520 total spend. That one list netted me over $250,000 annually for more than five years.

It was not expensive or complicated to make. I'll show you how.

I've helped hundreds of other companies and small business owners do the same thing.

2 – Free Offer

Give them something insanely valuable for free in exchange for their name and email address.

The key here is to understand your ideal buyer's "Transformational Journey", i.e. the journey they are on to find a trusted source to solve their problem or fulfill their deepest desires.

You need to invest some of your best thinking and give some of your best value on the Free Offer. This will establish your relationship with your ideal buyer and dramatically increase your future conversion rates.

3 – Low-Cost Offer

The moment they accept your Free Offer, you will invite them to buy something from you.

This will be something that is very inexpensive for them. In some cases, your ideal buyers might have a high emotional price threshold and you can offer something that is over $100.

But, for the vast majority of people selling a digital product, the low-cost initial offer should be under $10. In all my testing, I have found that $7 has the best conversion rate.

This offer should also be insanely valuable to them. It should be worth at least $100+... in other words, it should be selling at a 90%-95% discount.

4 – In-Cart Bump Offer

When you sell your Low-Cost Offer, you will include an in-cart Bump Offer on the checkout page.

The price point will be $19, or almost 3x the price of the initial offer. Over time, you can test other price points, but this has proven to be the most universally effective.

Your Bump Offer will give them something in the same desired category. In other words, if they got a free download to get secrets on losing weight, your Low-Cost Offer and your in-cart Bump Offers will give them additional ways to lose weight.

The difference is the consumption modality. I'll give you a detailed list of different modalities you can use as a Bump Offer in Chapter 6.

5 – Follow-Up Emails

The reality is, your initial conversion rates for the Low-Cost Offer will be under 8%. Most of my clients are delighted if they can get above 2%.

The easiest way to push that conversion rate to around 7%-10% is to create a follow-up sequence.

Your Low-Cost Offer follow-up sequence will be three emails, where you simply give them reasons to buy and a deadline.

6 – One-Time Offer

The moment they accept your Low-Cost Offer, you will present them with a One-Time Offer.

Typically, this is an upsell offer that sells for around 5-7 times the Low-Cost Offer. You will create an offer for $37

They will purchase this with a one-click button, meaning the buyer does not need to enter their contact or payment information again—they just click and the purchase is made.

One-Time Offers can get very complicated. In the future, you can add upsells (higher cost than the initial purchase), downsells (lower price than the upsell... not the initial purchase), and neutral sells (around the same price as the initial purchase). For now, you'll just have a single One-Time Offer to keep it simple.

7 – "Thank You" Page Offer

After your ideal buyer goes through the funnel sequence of Free >> Low-Cost Offer >> One-Time Offer, you will direct them to the "Thank You" Page.

On this page, you will give them one more offer. In this case, it will be another Free Offer positioned as a surprise gift.

For now, this will simply be a placeholder. As you get the funnel running smoothly and profitably, you will use this page to draw them into another funnel and offer.

8 – Fulfillment Emails

This is two types of emails.

The first is a single email. It is a Welcome Email, which thanks them and tells them how to access the product or service they just purchased. It is sent instantly.

The other emails are what we call "Consumption Emails". This is a series of 3-5 emails sent over 7-10 days. These emails inspire them to "consume" your Transformational Idea. You give them insights and best practices on making the most of your offer. You ask them to review their purchase, share their experience with you, resolve any concerns they might have, and post something nice about you on social media.

9 – Nurturing Email Sequence

I once attended a private mastermind group with Brendon Burchard. There were just eight people in the room. All of them (except me at the time) had large multi-million dollar businesses.

Brendon turned to one of them and said, "Did you write that Nurturing Sequence yet?" The girl looked rather bashful and said, "Not yet, but I will".

Brendon lovingly, but forcefully exploded, "That is worth several million dollars to you and will free up your time. It is only 11 emails. You have to promise me you'll do it by the end of next week!"

I had been writing and using email Nurturing Sequences for more than 10 years at that point and knew for a fact that Brendon was right.

Your sequence is 11 emails. They can be short—between 100 and 500 words each. They load up your ideal buyer with high-quality value, then makes an offer, then sets a deadline for them to accept the offer.

It is very simple, very profitable, and infinitely scalable… and sadly, it is one of the least utilized profit techniques in the business world.

Your Transformational Journey

If you don't fully understand the nine elements I just outlined, don't worry!

This book is all about walking you through each one. The bonus materials I've added give you tools and templates to rapidly put everything to profitable use.

You are on a transformative journey that will take you from having an idea that can change the world to seeing it become a reality and being put to use by your ideal buyers.

Highest Leverage Elements

As you look at those nine elements, you should ask yourself these questions:

"Which of the nine elements are the most important? Which ones make the biggest difference in profits and conversion rates?"

Before I give you the answer, let me tell you what the highest priority is for you at this stage of the game:

First and foremost, Rapid Return on Ad Spend (RROAS).

When you spend $10 on ads, how fast can you get your money back in the form of customer purchases?

120 days?

90 days?

60 days?

How about 10 minutes?

The faster you can get a return on your ad spend, the faster you can push out more ads. If you can get a faster return on your ad spend than your competitors, then you win. You now have the power to get in front of more of your ideal buyers more often.

Additionally, you have the power to extend your reach and go deeper into the pool of potential buyers.

I like virtually instant ROAS, but will accept as long as 30 days.

Later in your business development, you'll look at the inverse of this number... meaning, when your business is bigger, the other way you'll beat out the competition is to have the ability to have a longer ROAS.

Many of my major clients are comfortable with a 3-12 month ROAS period.

For now, the name of the game is SPEED! Put a dollar in and get it back as instantaneously as possible.

The second criterion that's extremely important is Initial Customer Value (ICV).

If it costs me $47 to acquire a customer, then initially, what is that customer worth to me?

If the ICV is $47, then I break even.

That's not bad—it's wonderful, in fact! I'm basically building a list of buyers for free. My big profits will come down the road from my Nurturing Sequences.

If the ICV is $27 and I've spent $47, then I've lost $20 and need to wait until more purchases are made to get a nice Return on Ad Spend (ROAS) and, eventually, profits.

But what if my ICV in this example could be $77?

That is just downright amazing. I put in $47 of advertising money and within a single funnel transaction set, I not only break even, but I have $30 of extra profits!

This allows me to create exponential growth. I can spend faster and spend more on client acquisition than my competitors.

And even if you're not concerned about competitors, these extra initial profits give you power to grow faster and faster. Your influence grows, your impact grows, and your sense of fulfillment and joy grows.

So, which of the nine funnel elements are the highest leverage? Which of these are most important to give you a Rapid Return on Ad Spend (under 30 days) and increase your Initial Customer Value?

Here they are, listed in order of importance and impact:

6 – One-Time Offer (OTO)

A buyer is most likely to buy when they have just made a purchase.

One-Time Offer conversion rates can be as high as 40% when crafted and priced correctly (I show you exactly how to do this in Chapter 5).

If your initial offer is $7 and your OTO is $37 and 40% of your buyers get it, then your average Initial Customer Value is now $21.80... or three times what it would be without a One-Time Offer.

Typically, customer acquisition costs for most people in this space is around $30-$50 when they just start out. So, with one offer, you have almost instantly broken even on your ad spend... and that's before doing anything else.

It is very powerful.

4 – In-Cart Bump Offer

This instantly gives you an extra $19. If you have a 20% conversion rate on your Bump Offer, that means you just raised your Initial Customer Value by $4.75. This is not trivial. It represents half a day of advertising money if you set a daily budget of $10. You just increased your reach and influence by 50%.

But, more important than the extra money, the additional purchase is proven to make the buyer more apt to buy more.

Yes, just by including a Bump Offer, you increase conversion rates on your One-Time Offer, your "Thank You" Page Offer, and the offer you put in your Nurturing Sequence.

If you do it right, and depending on your Customer Acquisition Cost, you could almost instantly break even on your ad spend with just the Bump Offer and One-Time Offer. Many of my clients do exactly that... as do I personally when running funnels for my companies.

5 – Follow-Up Emails

As a reminder, this is just three emails.

They are automatically activated when a buyer does not buy the Low-Cost Offer or the One-Time Offer.

Follow-up emails typically double or triple conversion rates... and almost no one uses them. But you will.

The follow-up emails simply put a 48-hour deadline on accepting the deals you've offered them. They get one on day one and two on day two. Easy, short, and sweet.

9 – Nurturing Sequence

The other three elements (6, 4, and 5) are magical at helping you realize a rapid return on ad spend. They increase instant, initial customer value.

The Nurturing Sequence takes a little longer to do its job. Specifically, this sequence will run for seven days and include 11 emails.

Conversion rates, especially for the first sequence, can be as high as 50%. This is the heavyweight champion of increasing Initial Customer Value... even if you have to wait a week to get your money.

The reason is because you are now operating from a position of trust and working with known buyers.

Additionally, many people who got your Free Offer, but did not purchase your Low-Cost Offer or One-Time Offer, have now had time to digest your material, experience some results, and get to know you a little better.

They are now exponentially more likely to buy from you and it will show up in your sales.

CHAPTER 2

Tools Only Used by Professionals

I shot to my feet like I'd been bit in the behind by a crocodile.

"I get it now! I see it all! I can't believe what they've been doing to me all these years! I thought it was so complicated and needed a dozen super expensive software programs. But it doesn't! I see it all now!"

I was practically shouting. My breathing came in heaves and my heart was racing. I spun around and faced Perry.

"How long have you known all this? I can't believe I'm just seeing all this now! It's so simple!"

I spun around to the other three men sitting in Perry's comfortable home office. Throwing my hands in the air, I said, "Did you guys know all this? You know what they've been doing to me all these years? It's incredible! I can't believe I never saw it!"

When I was done with my rant, the room went oddly quiet. Perry and the others simply stared at me in amazement.

Slowly, a big smile spread across their faces. Perry began to laugh.

"Guys, I think Joshua just had a breakthrough. What do you guys think?"

They all laughed.

"Yes, Joshua, it is exciting when you figure out how all this comes together. You did kind of interrupt what I was saying to Steve. We can chat about your revelation a little later. Cool?"

I agreed and slowly sat back down.

For the past two days, the four of us had been working with Perry on our businesses. It was a rapid-fire problem/solution session. We presented business challenges to Perry and he helped us solve them.

With each solution, I would see another piece of the marketing and sales funnel system drop into place.

Finally, toward the end of the second day, it all came together. I saw it all with perfect clarity. It hit me so forcefully that I jumped up and interrupted the meeting.

For years, I had searched for information online—information about a zillion things.

How to plant a vegetable garden.

How to lay tiles.

How to use super glue to close up a wound instead of paying a doctor a thousand bucks to put a few stitches in. (Hey, important info when you have five high-energy boys in a row.)

How to get ripped abs with a sweet six-pack. (Still working on that one!)

How to write a book.

And on and on.

Like you, I love learning and doing new things.

I was always amazed how I'd start out looking for a bit of information... and somehow, a few hours later... be sucked into buying all kinds of products, how-to guides, and services.

How did THEY do it to me?

What systems did THEY use to pull me in and suck money out of my wallet?

It was always a mystery to me... but then, suddenly, it was 100% clear.

One of the biggest revelations was the structure of the funnel and the tools marketers used to make it all work online.

Just like with any business, you're going to need some specific tools. Each tool will cost you money. They will be relatively small investments that, when used correctly, will bring you a return totally disproportionate to the money spent.

For example, one of our clients spends less than $300 a month for a complete online sales platform, but they use this platform to generate several million dollars in sales.

You can do the same.

To follow the steps I outline in this book, you will need the following resources and digital tools.

A Transformational Idea

The first resource you'll need is an outline of the Transformational Journey you offer your target audience.

In simple terms, you need to answer three questions:

1. What major problem or desire does my ideal buyer have?
2. What is my solution?
3. Why should they buy from me instead of someone else?
4. The answers to these three questions will help you create ads and the different offers you'll make to your buyers.

The main cost to this is your time.

I strongly suggest that you set aside 3-8 hours of isolated time to really articulate this. You probably already have it in your head, but put it in writing so you can strengthen and refine it.

If you need help working on this, there is a best-practices guide in your bonus materials.

A Simple Website

You need a basic, simple website.

For the purposes of this book, I'm going to assume that you have a website. In truth, you can do everything outlined in this book with a one-page website. It is better to have all the elements I've outlined below, but a single page will do the trick.

If you don't have a website right now, we can build you a professional site in a few days, with all the elements you need. Contact us at website@strahes.com or www.Strahes.com/website for details.

For your reference, here's a simple outline of what elements you should include on your website:

- **Homepage** - On the homepage, your copy should identify: 1 – Who your ideal buyer is. 2 – the main challenge/desire you're addressing. 3 – Your solution. 4 – Access to your funnel via an opt-in form.
- **About You** - This page should be a story that helps them emotionally connect with you and trust you. It should not be a biography or resume.
- **Services/Solution** - This is an entry point for your funnel. It should outline the problem/desire of your ideal buyer and get them started on consuming your solution. Usually, this means having an opt-in form.
- **Testimonials** - A simple page that has a few testimonials or case studies about your solution. In the beginning, you need 3-5.

- **Contact Us** - A contact form so your ideal buyer can reach out to you. It is good to also include an opt-in form to help them enter your funnel.

Again, if you are not careful, this one step could cost you the whole game.

I attended a seminar 15 years ago and was told I needed a website to build my business.

I agreed, and four weeks later, using a template and my knowledge of HTML coding, I had a simple website.

About 10 years later, and after making a small fortune from that site, I ran into someone who had been at the conference with me.

"How's business going?" I asked.

"Pretty good. I'm still working on rolling things out. In fact, my latest website is just about done. It's getting close so I can start selling."

I've seen it hundreds of times... people try to take the cheap route on this step and do the website themselves... only to spend weeks or months or years working on it and getting it just right. The reality is, you just need to get it done and over with.

By far the best way to make it happen is to hire a professional to help you and focus on the funnel that will bring your Transformational Idea to millions of people.

CRM/Funnel Builder Platform

CRM stands for Customer Relationship Manager.
You will need the ability to:

- Create opt-in forms to give buyers access to your funnel.
- Automatically redirect your buyer to different pages and offers based on their actions. For example, when they sign

up for your Free Offer, they need to be directed to your Low-Cost Offer, and so on...

- Collect and safely store contact and payment information.
- Track IP addresses, purchase history, etc., so you know exactly what your buyers have done in your world.
- Build digital products, product pages, and order forms so you can collect payment information for both static orders and subscriptions.
- Host videos, audio files, and images.
- Manage subscriptions.
- Allow customers to automatically cancel or upgrade their orders and subscriptions.
- Automatically follow up when your customers buy or don't buy.
- Write and safely send emails, manually and automatically based on buyer behavior.

There are a TON of CRM systems out there, but most of them are partial solutions or overly complicated.

In my experience, working with thousands of entrepreneurs and hundreds of CRM/Funnel systems, there are only four systems that I would recommend.

The best option on the market today is a company called Kartra. I recommend that you use Kartra to build the system outlined in this book. It will dramatically simplify things for you.

Kartra has everything you need and is extremely reasonably priced.

As an added bonus, Kartra is the easiest to learn and fastest to implement for beginners.

Kartra costs between $99 and $499, depending on which level you need.

If the technical setup of a CRM intimidates you or if you don't really want to spend your time doing that part of the process because your time is too valuable, then we can take this off your hands. We offer done-for-you Kartra services, including complete funnel buildout based on the exact steps in this book.

To learn more about our funnel done-for-you service, contact us at: funnel@strahes.com or www.Strahes.com/funnel

The second option is ClickFunnels. It is more complicated than Kartra and has much less base functionality. However, it has more users than Kartra and a little better support, both from the company and from the community.

ClickFunnels costs between $81 and $297 a month, but to get some of the same features found in Kartra, you need to purchase additional add-ons, making it potentially very expensive.

The third option is Kajabi. Kajabi is less sophisticated and comprehensive than Kartra and ClickFunnels.

Kajabi costs between $119 and $319 a month. Like ClickFunnels, you need to keep an eye on the limits for each level and the add-ons you may need.

Facebook Ads Account

You will do paid advertising.

This means you'll need a Facebook (now Meta) Ads account.

The good news is that you can get set up for advertising for free, and it only takes a few minutes.

Plan on spending about $10 a day in ads, or about $300 a month, to get started.

Remember, if you follow the system in this book, you will likely recoup that money almost instantly... or within a few weeks of investing it.

This means you can start building your list and making sales without any out-of-pocket expenses. We charge our ads on a credit card and pay it off weekly with revenues generated from your funnel.

As your ads and funnel improve, you'll be more confident in your Return on Ad Spend and can increase this budget. The more you spend, the faster your business grows (again... when you manage it the right way).

We'll address best practices for your Facebook Ads in later chapters.

You might also wonder about YouTube, Google, Instagram, Twitter, LinkedIn, and the other couple thousand platforms you could use for advertising.

Don't worry about all that right now. You don't need it to get started.

Finally, no doubt you've heard of "Content Marketing". It is often boasted of as a "free" way to get tons of traffic and sales. The hard reality is that content marketing is very complicated and takes a lot of time—sometimes years to really start producing the desired results. It is far from "free".

However, when done right, it is incredibly effective and you will definitely want to engage in content marketing... but down the road. Again, we are looking for speed and quick profits right now. Stay focused!

Checklist and Summary

To successfully follow the guidelines of this book and start making money in the next 30-60 days, you'll need:

- ☐ **A Value Proposition** – What value do you provide to your ideal customer? Set aside 3-8 hours of isolated time to really articulate this. You probably already have it in your head, but put it in writing so you can strengthen and refine it. Estimated Costs: 3-8 hours of your time.

- ☐ **A Simple Website** – If you don't already have a website, you'll need a simple site to implement everything in this book. To save time, you should outsource it. It shouldn't take more than a week—two at the most—to have your website up and running. Contact us for help with building your site quickly so you can start selling ASAP.

- ☐ **CRM/Funnel Builder Platform** – In my experience, the best option on the market today is a company called Kartra. It has everything you need. It's also the easiest to learn and fastest to implement for beginners. Other options include ClickFunnels, Kajabi, and Keep. Estimated Costs: between $99 and $999

- ☐ **Facebook (Meta) Ads** – It's totally free and just takes a few minutes to open a Meta Business Suite account so you can run ads. Remember, if you follow this system, it is likely you will recoup that money almost instantly... or within a few weeks of investing it. Estimated Costs: $100-$300/month to get started.

Phase One: Meet

In Phase One: Meet, you are meeting a new buyer for the first time. They know nothing about you. Never heard your name. Wouldn't know you from Adam if they ran into you at the store.

You need to introduce yourself and make it worthwhile for them to get to know you a little better.

The meet phase plays several extremely important roles.

Become a Bridge Builder

First, in Phase One, your ideal buyer comes to know you and begins to trust you.

The trust comes from you understanding the ideal buyer well enough that you know what they need, right when they need it. In this way, you are a "Bridge Builder".

Companies that stand the test of time and continue to scale up year after year have a clear vision of who their customers are and what is coming down the road for them.

I'm reminded of the poem, *The Bridge Builder* by Will Allen Dromgoole:

> An old man going a lone highway,
> Came, at the evening cold and gray,
> To a chasm vast and deep and wide.

Through which was flowing a sullen tide
The old man crossed in the twilight dim,
The sullen stream had no fear for him;
But he turned when safe on the other side
And built a bridge to span the tide.

"Old man," said a fellow pilgrim near,
"You are wasting your strength with building here;
Your journey will end with the ending day,
You never again will pass this way;
You've crossed the chasm, deep and wide,
Why build this bridge at evening tide?"

The builder lifted his old gray head;
"Good friend, in the path I have come," he said,
"There followed after me to-day
A youth whose feet must pass this way.
This chasm that has been as naught to me
To that fair-haired youth may a pitfall be;
He, too, must cross in the twilight dim;
Good friend, I am building this bridge for him!"

We are the bridge builders, building products, services, tools, courses, and systems to help our fellow man in their journey. Let me give an example of how successful companies do this.

In March 2006, I sat at my computer writing a long-copy sales letter. I was a new freelance copywriter and this was one of my first major projects. I was almost $200,000 in debt with minimal income to feed my large family of seven. I needed the $5,000 and future commissions this letter would bring.

My screen flickered and then turned solid blue 15 pages into the sales letter. The infamous Microsoft Windows Blue Screen of Death struck. Sadly, in those days, the "cloud" didn't exist... and I did not have autosave set up.

I lost 12 pages of copy and had to start all over. I have never been more frustrated in my life.

I picked up the phone and called my geek brother, Jacob.

"My computer just crashed and I need a new one. It has to be one that I can trust and will not die on me. What do you recommend?"

"Meet me down at the Apple store. We'll get you a new iMac."

That began a mild obsession with Apple products. Today, in my immediate family, we have eight iMac computers, 13 iPads, six Apple Watches, 15 iPhones, and subscriptions to all the services.

At each stage of our lives, we've found that there is an Apple product or service waiting there for us to solve a problem, enjoy a better lifestyle, or feel geeky and cool.

For us, and millions of others, Apple has been a Bridge Builder, anticipating our needs and being a company we can trust.

This is not an Apple infomercial... but the point is this...

Map out the hopes, wishes, desires, and needs of your ideal buyer. Be the kind of company that they can trust. Grow with them. Help them along the way. They will reward you with an ever-increasing Lifetime Customer Value.

Salting the Oats

Second, by building trust, you begin a process I call, "Salting the Oats".

"Salting the Oats" is a pre-suasion process that predisposes buyers to like you, want to be around you, want to listen to you, and ultimately, want to buy from you... again and again and again.

You remember the old expression... "You can lead a horse to water but you can't make it drink."

PHASE ONE: MEET

While it's true that you can't make that horse drink from your water, you can put a wee bit of salt in the oats. This makes the horse thirsty and eager to drink when they get close to water.

You can do the same with your buyers. You cannot force or manipulate people into buying from you. But you can discover exactly what they perceive as important and valuable and place it persuasively in their path.

Help them see that you understand them and have exactly what they want. Gain their trust, and you'll have a loyal, happy buyer for life.

The first step—the "salt"—is valuable content that solves a challenge for them and fulfills an immediate desire.

Inside this section, we will cover the two things you need in Phase One:

1. **A Free Offer** – Your Free Offer is the fastest, most effective way you can help your ideal buyer see results on their journey.
2. **Paid Ads** – Paid Ads are the way you instantly and consistently get access to millions of your ideal buyers.

In the following chapters, we cover exact details on building your Free Offer and creating ads that convert at a high level.

CHAPTER 3

How to Grab and Hold Attention

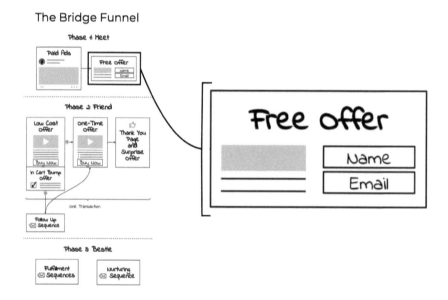

My head jerked around and my eyes instantly focused on a green sign about 100 yards down the road.

I had the odd sensation that someone had manually grabbed my head in their hands and forced me to look to the right. A voice inside my head said, "Look at that, now!" and my eyes involuntarily obeyed.

Driving on Interstate 64 on the south side of St. Louis, MO, there were plenty of things to look at.

Billboards.

Thousands of cars.

Massive skyscrapers and an endless sea of condos, apartments, and shops.

In addition to all of these visual cues, my ears were filled with sounds of my family in the car... children chattering, music, the roar of road noise.

It was a high-input environment with millions of data points for my mind to process.

There were so many things I could have focused my mind on—not the least of which was staying safe while traveling at 75mph down the freeway!

So, why, in the middle of this insanely busy environment, did my mind suddenly force me to involuntarily look at one small sign on the side of the road—a green sign no bigger than two feet by four feet?

The answer holds the secret to creating a Free Offer that will consistently convert and bring your ideal buyers to you.

Inside your brain, there is something called the Reticular Activating System, or RAS for short.

This system controls data flow between your conscious and subconscious mind. Among other things, it determines what is important enough for your conscious mind to focus on.

Everything around you—every bit of data collected by your senses—passes through your RAS and instantly gets labeled as "important" or "unimportant".

This is why, when you're scrolling through emails, you automatically ignore 95% of them... but then suddenly, there's that one that seems to jump off the page at you and grab your attention. You spend time reading it and, if it is interesting enough, you do something about it.

What was the sign that grabbed my attention that day in St. Louis?

It was a sign that said, "Town and Country City Limits".

Why was that important to me?

I was driving a Chrysler Town and Country van. Because my family was in that van and because I'd spent money on the car, my brain had stored away that Town and Country was important to me.

So, when my eyes saw the sign, my RAS fired and forced me to pay attention.

Your job is to understand your ideal buyer so well that you know what their mind labels as important and then put it in front of them over and over again.

Your ads and your Free Offer need to be filled with RAS Triggers.

By doing this, you literally hijack your ideal buyer's mind and get them to involuntarily ignore everything else and pay attention to you.

RAS Triggers can be fired by words, images, sounds, smells, or feelings.

In our efforts to help you get results fast, we will focus on using words and then images.

Here are a few examples of high-pulling ads and offers. Look at the words they use and think of how that lights up the brain of their ideal buyer to pay attention:

Moms

> The hardest job in the world.
> Is the best job in the world.
> Thank you, Mom.

An ad for Proctor and Gamble products. Anyone with a job and a mom is suddenly paying attention, right? Proctor and Gamble make more than a dozen household brands such as Tide, Vicks, Downey, Gillette, and many others.

Stuff mothers use every day.

Personal Development

> Why do some people have so much CONFIDENCE? 🤔
> Most people believe their confidence is based on luck or how they were raised...
> Confidence Masterclass

Brendon Burchard is targeting people interested in personal development. He begins with a question that his ideal buyer regularly asks themselves. He continues with a statement of belief that is going on inside their head.

He knows they want more confidence and believes that more confidence will help them be more successful in life.

Investment Newsletters

> The End of America

That is the tagline of one of the most successful direct-response pieces ever written. Stansberry Research released this as a long-copy sales letter. Released in 2011, the target audience was investors facing growing inflation and financial troubles in the US.

Many of them already believed that the US Dollar was in trouble. This headline gave voice to their fears and grabbed their attention.

But grabbing attention is only part of the battle.

Once you have their attention, you need to hold it. You do this by healing "the bleeding neck".

Identify the "Bleeding Neck"

The "bleeding neck" can be a serious challenge your ideal buyer is facing, or an intense desire they have.

Here's an example of an urgent challenge I had...

I once had a last-minute opportunity to do a presentation and sell my services at a large business conference. The organizers insisted I use PowerPoint slides. I know the content that a sales presentation needs, but I'm not skilled at all in the creative and design department. I only had three days to get it all done.

I jumped online, searched for slide templates and best practices on how to make it look good, quickly. I found a free online guide that gave me a great outline, including screenshots and examples.

After putting in my name and email, I downloaded the guide. I gave it a quick skim and realized I really didn't have time to do all of this.

Gratefully, the guy who created the guide also did done-for-you services. His contact information was on every page of the guide.

I contacted him and asked him to crank out the design for me. He agreed. I paid nearly three times the normal rates for a rush job and got it done.

The presentation went extremely well. I closed almost $200,000 in sales—way more than I paid on the slide rush job!

I used that designer a number of times after that and referred dozens of people to him.

In a minute, I'll show you how to identify the "bleeding neck" and create quick-win solutions for your ideal buyer.

Create an Information Product

The thing that earned that graphic designer tens of thousands of dollars from me and my referrals was the free guide he wrote on PowerPoint slide best practices.

Your first project is to create a Free Offer that will entice people to give you their name and email address.

This is the first major step in your relationship with them.

As a general rule, your Free Offer should tell people WHAT to do, not HOW to do it.

For example, for years, one of my companies, CopywriterMarketer, has offered a report called, "10 Predictors of Success as a Freelance Copywriter". Inside, it details the top 10 things writers can focus on to be successful. It is a relatively short report and omits detailed instructions on how to do each thing.

Here's another way to look at this. Have you ever taken your car in for a brake inspection?

I've done this—the technician inspected my brakes for free. Then he came back with a list of parts and labor needed to fix my brakes. "You'll need new calipers, pads, and rotors. Plus, you'll need to flush the lines and put new brake fluid in."

He told me exactly what I needed to do, but did not tell me how to do it.

If I was a savvy DIY car repair guy, I could've taken my car home and fixed it right up. OR... handed the guy a credit card and told him to do it... which is what I did.

The highest leverage types of free things you can offer are:

- **Cheat Sheets** – One or two pages of some of the best information, actionable strategies, and resources you can squeeze in there.
- **10 Reasons Why** – Or other kinds of valuable lists. The lists can give actionable details that bring results. Again, focus on telling them WHAT to do, not exactly HOW to do it.
- **Books** – Book offers are incredibly successful. You can offer an eBook or a physical book where they pay for shipping. Perry Marshall, Brendon Burchard, Dean Graziosi, Russell Brunson, and others have added millions of people to their tribe using this method.

- **Whitepapers** – If you are in a technology space, a well-written whitepaper can be incredibly successful.
- **Trial Offer** – This is the top offer for most SaaS companies. Let them get in and use the software. Open up the premium version so they see and experience it all.

NOTE: To keep things simple, in our process, you will create a Cheat Sheet. As you get comfortable making Free Offers, you can come back and repeat the process with some of the other types of Free Offers.

Pro-Tips for Free Offers:
- **Instant Gratification** – Make your offer instant gratification. If their deepest desire is like an itch that is driving them crazy, think about how you can scratch that itch instantly.
- **Jargon Rich** – Understand the language our idea buyer uses to describe their challenges and desires. Use their language, not yours.
- **Social Proof** – Include social proof elements. Nowhere is social proof needed more than on the initial Free Offer.
- **Two Steps** – Include a two-step process. Remember that micro-commitments win the day. If you are asking them for detailed contact information, make the first step a simple "Enter your name and email to get started" type of form. Then take them to the full contact form.

There are eight steps to creating your Cheat Sheet Free Offer:

1. Define the Deliverable
2. Choose the Format
3. Create the Free Offer
4. Format and Shine It Up
5. Set Up Your Free Offer in the CRM

6. Create the Opt-In Form and Page
7. Create the "Thank You" Page
8. Write the Welcome and Fulfillment Email

Let's go through each step so you have a clear idea of what needs to be done, what costs are involved, and how long it will take.

1 – Define the Deliverable

As I stated before, the most important thing you can do is identify the urgent challenge they need solved or desire they want fulfilled.

I use a simple, four-question process to identify the "bleeding neck".

Set aside 3-4 hours of time so you can focus, research, record, and get clarity on these four questions.

For example, you might look at the first question and say, "I'm not totally clear what the top challenge is for my ideal buyer!" To discover that, you can read industry websites, talk to your ideal buyer and interview them, or read conversations in online groups.

I once did a marketing project targeting forensic police chiefs. I called over 50 police departments around the country and talked with forensic police officers about their biggest challenges. It didn't take long before I really understood them.

Here are the questions you should ask and answer to help you create your Free Offer:

- What challenge or desire can I solve for my ideal buyer?
- If the solution to their total challenge is a journey of 10 steps, what is the first step?
- How can I help them take that first step with a single, simple action and help them get instant or almost instant results?

- Why, with all the other solutions and options out there, would they pay attention to my offer and want to give me their name and email address?

Once you have the answers to these questions, answer this one last question:

- What single outcome can I help them realize for a "quick-win"?

The answer to this question is the big idea and main persuasion point to your Free Offer.

A key point here… in almost all of your Free Offers, you will focus on telling them WHAT to do… not HOW to do it.

We will talk about this more in Chapter 5, but think of it like this…

I could say to you, "To be successful and make a lot of money, you need to build a funnel. The funnel has nine major elements…" I could go on and tell you all about the nine elements and why they are important.

Now you know WHAT to do, but there are a lot of details missing, right? I've given you value, and if you already know what a landing page, Bump Offer, and One-Time Offer are, you could create a successful funnel.

But, if those are new terms to you, then you'll need more details on exactly HOW to make all that stuff work.

To get those details, you'd buy this book! This book shows you both what to do and how to do it.

But, a Free Offer should stop at telling your ideal buyer what to do.

2 – Choose the Format

As I mentioned before, I suggest you keep this simple and select the Cheat Sheet format for building out your funnel.

A simple Cheat Sheet can be used in any industry, is quick to produce, and has high value.

In the event that you have resources or a desire to do something in addition to the Cheat Sheet, here is a list of the different formats you can use...

- **Cheat Sheet** – This is usually a one-page document crammed with a ton of best practice ideas on it. The key to the Cheat Sheet is organized, high-leverage information. Give them as much as possible in as little space as possible.
- **Written Report or Guide** – Write it up, add some pictures, format it like a guide or a book, publish it as a PDF, and you're done! This should be between two and 10 pages. Make it easy to consume with large fonts, pictures, and white space.
- **Video Mini-Course** – This is typically 3-5 videos, between 3-10 minutes each. The flow is something like this:
  - Video 1: Overview and Summary
  - Videos 2-3: Teaching Points
  - Final Video: Conclusion and Next Steps
- **Audio Mini-Course** – This is identical to a video course but without the video. A key point here is to include an introduction and some music at the beginning, between segments, and at the end.
- **Whitepaper** – This is a technical document that details pros and cons of specific technology solutions. If you are in a technology space, a well-written whitepaper can be incredibly successful.
- **Simple Ebook** – This can be an insider's guide into a common challenge your ideal buyer has. I wrote one years ago when I was a new freelance copywriter trying to land projects. It was

called "Copy Revolution: The Personalities of Copywriting".. It was about 45 pages. I sent out hundreds of these in PDF format and landed dozens of clients from it.
- **Trial Offer** – This is the top offer for most SaaS companies. Let them get in and use the software. Open up the premium version so they see and experience it all.

See examples in your bonus materials.

Here's a pro-tip...

I strongly recommend that your Free Offer format is a Cheat Sheet or a Written Report of some kind.

The reason for this is that it is easy for people to quickly skim a written report and get value from it. Video is an extremely popular communication format, but you might be surprised to learn two facts...

First, email is still the #1 communication method in the world.

Second, upwards of 90% of all videos watched have the sound off... meaning people just look at them and read the subtitles, if the video has them. Yes, people are reading their videos!

When you want quick information and solutions, nothing beats zipping through a written report to digest it at a glance.

3 – Create the Free Offer

Once you know the deliverable and the format, you need to set aside time to actually create your Free Offer.

The most effective way to do this is to create dedicated, non-negotiable appointments for yourself.

Here's what a dedicated, non-negotiable appointment looks like...

My good friend and long-time business partner, Susan Kuse, had a bad knee. For years, it caused her pain and eventually got worse and worse. She finally saw an orthopedic surgeon and scheduled a knee replacement.

The surgery date was scheduled three months out. Every day of those three months was intensely painful for her.

Let me ask you this... what do you think would have had to happen for her to miss that surgery date?

As she said to me, "Someone in my family would need to be dying or dead. Nothing else would keep me from getting my knee done."

Once you have the time dedicated, here is a framework for how to actually go about creating the Free Offer.

1 – Create an Outline

Whichever format you've chosen, you'll need a written outline. Here's a template you can work off of:

1. **Key Benefits and Deliverables** – What's in it for them? What will the end result of this free gift be for them? How will they grow in their health, wealth, or relationships?
2. **Overview** – A few bullet points on the actual content and what they will learn.
3. **Action Steps** – Details on the action steps you recommend for them. A great idea is to think of your solution as a journey. Make it 3, 5, or 10 steps. The shorter the better. Remember, this is "Quick Win" material. The point is to stop the "bleeding neck" as soon as possible.
4. **Conclusion and Next Steps** – Wrap things up by summarizing your solution and give them clear next steps to take.

Plan on spending no more than five hours on the outline. If you're like most human beings on the planet, you will write most effectively in 45-60 minute blocks with 5-10 minute breaks.

Depending on your schedule, you can book one five-hour appointment with yourself and break it up into five sessions... or book five one-hour appointments.

But, it is vital to book out the time. Set that appointment and be committed to yourself. This is NON-NEGOTIABLE time.

One other pro-tip...

You'll be twice as effective if you set a specific goal and give yourself a little reward for hitting that goal.

For example, you could say, "My goal is to get my outline done in four hours. If I do, I'll treat myself to some Bluebell Ice Cream!" (Or whatever small reward trips your trigger! I used to reward myself by reading a Dr. Suess book to one of our young children. Very inspiring!)

2 – Write it!

Once you have the outline, it is time to actually write it out. Here are some suggestions based on your Free Offer format:

- **Cheat Sheet or Written Report** – You need to actually write it out, word-for-word.
- **Video and Audio** – When I do video and audio, I simply use the outline and talk about each point. I'm comfortable with this and have done it for years. If you're not comfortable with on-the-fly live production, you'll need to write out a script. If you do a complete script, it is important that you practice reading it so it sounds natural and engaging.

Your Free Offer is very important and deserves your best efforts... and it needs to get done. Don't take too much time or get overly obsessed with this. It will never be perfect. It needs to be good enough.

It is the foundation for your other offers. Think of it as a seed that, when planted, will quickly spring up into a fruitful tree that will give you fruit for many years to come.

Like with the outline, it is vital that you set a number of non-negotiable appointments with yourself. This is $10,000 per hour work and deserves your focus.

#3 – Peer Review It

One of the most important things you can do is have other people review your report. Too often, we get stuck in our own echo chamber. We need other people's insights, wisdom, and inspiration on our work.

Elon Musk is famous for seeking out the most critical people he can find to blow holes in his ideas and work.

Be willing to do the same.

Have the courage to seek out feedback.

The best way to do this is to ask the following groups of people to review your work:

- **Your Ideal Buyer** – Find two or three people that are your target audience. Ask them to review it for content. Is it interesting and desirable to them?
- **Professional Editors** – Ask a pro to proofread it and make sure it is grammatically correct.
- **The Disconnected** – Find two or three people who are totally disconnected from your ideal buyer group. Ask them to read it for clarity. Does it make sense? Can they follow your ideas, even if they don't understand them?

4 – Format and Shine it Up

The level of professional formatting and shininess depends on your audience.

I remember years ago, when I was in my early 20s, going to a Chinese buffet restaurant with my boss and mentor, Lennon. We were traveling together and found the closest thing we could to eat and run. The Chinese buffet was quick, cheap, and relatively healthy.

Lennon was a mild neat freak and loved things clean and orderly.

The restaurant was anything but shiny-clean. Oil on the floor. Dirty benches and chairs. An odd odor that lingered under the smells of soy sauce and sweet & sour chicken.

Lennon was also fairly outspoken. He demanded to see the manager. The manager was also the owner. When he came to our table, Lennon said, "I run several successful businesses. If you cleaned this place up a little better, you would make a lot more money. Customers would be much happier eating here."

The owner, a short weather-wrinkled Chinese man, shook his head emphatically, "No! If I clean, no best customers come."

I was shocked until I looked around the restaurant and then out the window. Both Lennon and I failed to notice that we were in a lower-income side of town. The hard reality was that people on this side of town were used to things being a little run-down and a little messy. It was their comfort zone.

The owner was right. If he cleaned his place up and made it all ship-shape-shiny, his best customers would feel uncomfortable and stop coming.

Now, I'm not suggesting you make your Free Offer unprofessional and sloppy. But I am suggesting you understand your ideal buyer well enough to know how polished this needs to be.

For example, if your ideal buyer is very personable and genuine, your video could be nothing more than you grabbing a smartphone and hitting record. Lighting and audio can be OK, and final editing could be close to zero.

On the other hand, if your ideal buyer is used to the finer things in life, you need to take time to make sure image quality is top-level, sound is clear, and lighting is bright. Formatting should include B-roll images, charts, a classy opening and ending, and some music.

Again, it all depends on your ideal buyer's comfort zone.

Here's a pro-tip…

If your ideal buyer needs a high level of shiny, then you're probably wise to outsource this, unless you have document, video, and/or audio editing skills. Hire someone who has a great eye for detail and creativity. It will cost you between $100 and $1000, but it will be well worth it.

If your shiny level does not resonate with your ideal buyer's comfort zone, you will repel them and ruin your sales and profits… no matter how good your content is.

Remember, people DO judge the book by the cover. Never let aesthetics distract from your message. Instead, make it support and strengthen your message.

5 – Set Up Your Free Offer in the CRM

It is time to get your Free Offer set up inside your CRM.

If you use Kartra or ClickFunnels, we offer a detailed, step-by-step, over-the-shoulder video training on exactly how to do everything you need to build your funnel. You can get more information on this inside your Bonus Membership.

Most CRMs will have a workflow similar to this:

1. Create your offer
2. Write a short description
3. Add any images, like boxshots or cover images
4. Add to a membership or a resource page where the buyer can access it. You will send people to this page to access their video or report download once they sign up. Your CRM should make this simple for you.

5. Publish
6. Plan on taking no more than an hour to get this done. The CRM should do most of the heavy lifting for you.

This is another step that you can—and often should—outsource, especially if you're not overly technically savvy. You're not getting paid to do tech stuff. Your profits will come from giving value to others through your information. Don't get caught up being a designer or CRM engineer if you can avoid it.

Here's a pro-tip...

The description should be very benefit-driven. Remember, every word they read should add increased persuasion to the process.

Your product description here is no different. It should be a mini-benefit statement that has them nodding their heads and thinking, "I'm so glad I'm getting this!"

6 – Create the Opt-In Form and Page

Like with everything in this book, be aware that there are thousands of ways you could build an Opt-In Form and Landing Page.

But, I am going to give you one specific way to do it. It is simple, fast to set up, and proven to perform.

The format and design are important, but not nearly as important as the Transformational Idea. When you have a great idea and clearly communicate that, people will happily sign up.

The Opt-In Form

The Opt-In Form is the form they fill out to get your Free Offer. Typically, this form includes just two fields:

- First Name
- Email Address

Make both of these fields required.

At some point, you can also test these two optional fields:

- Last Name
- Phone Number

In some industries, these additional fields won't decrease conversion rates and may even improve overall Lifetime Customer Value.

But as a general rule, making the opt-in process more complicated in any way will decrease conversion ratios.

The title of your Free Offer is placed above the form and you should include some very short benefit-driven language.

The button should be large with an action verb and descriptive language such as: "Get My Report Now", "Sign Up Now", "Get Instant Access Now", "Download Now", etc.

You will use the Opt-In Form on your website's Home Page, Contact Us Page, at the bottom of the Testimonials and Services pages, and on your Opt-In Page.

> Here's a pro-tip... Include bright colors and graphics to draw attention, such as an arrow, stars, or a picture. If you use a picture of a person, be sure you can see the person's eyes and that they are relatable to your ideal buyer in terms of clothes, hair, gender, and race.

The Opt-In Page

This is a stand-alone page that you will drive ideal buyers to with your paid ads and, eventually, with other traffic sources.

It is sometimes called a "Landing Page" or a "Squeeze Page", but a more accurate way of thinking about it is an "Opt-In Page" because you are inviting your ideal buyer to be part of your world and giving them the power to say "yes" or "no".

You want your solution to be so relevant, so clear, so valuable to them that the only option that makes sense is to say "yes" and choose to be part of your world.

That is why you spend time focusing on giving value instead of thinking of ways to "trick" people into buying from you.

Your Opt-In Page has the following elements and copy:

- **⅔ Page Split Set Up** – Imagine your page divided into three parts horizontally. Your Headline and other copy will fill 2/3rds of the page, the Opt-In Form will fill the right-hand side 1/3rd of the page. In mobile mode, the headline will stay on top and the form will sit right under it, but above the other copy. The CRM will have templates that help make setup and design relatively easy.
- **Headline** – Attention-grabbing message, filled with a single, highly desirable promised benefit. In just a minute, I'll tell you all about the SAUCE method—a system to help you write highly persuasive headlines.
- **Opt-In Form** – This should be flushed right of the Headline and in line with it.
- **Compelling Image** – If appropriate, have an image of a person who is enjoying the benefits you're offering. Be sure the picture relates to your ideal buyer demographics. Have the person looking in the direction of the Opt-In Form.
- **Proof Elements** – Include social proof, stats, certifications, short quotes, or any other element that will prove you can deliver on your promises and build trust.
- **Sub-Head Line** – This goes under the Proof Elements and restates the promised benefit in the headline.

- **Main Body Copy** – This is a short paragraph further building on your promised benefit, followed by 3-5 bullet points describing what they get when they opt-in. The bullet points can contain some hints of the features and functions, i.e. "Inside your PDF report..." or, "At minute 2:38, you'll find...", but should mostly focus on an expansion of benefits. If you are promising them a way to lose weight, then you could include more details about why this is sure to help them. Examples of high-performing Opt-In Pages can be found in your bonus materials.
- **Testimonials** – Three to six testimonials that reinforce the promised benefits.
- **Final Call to Action and Form** – A final call to action. The easiest way to do this is to include a larger version of the Opt-In Form at the bottom of the page.

The #1 Secret to Improving Response Rates on Your Landing Page

The persuasion power of your copy – the messaging you use to convey your Transformational Idea and Offer is the most important thing about your landing page.

Nothing else will move the needle more than improving your copy.

So, let's spend a few minutes talking about copywriting secrets. We'll begin with a story about how I lost a persuasion battle to my six-year-old daughter...

When my daughter, Mary, was around six years old, we were standing in line at the grocery store. On our left were the usual shelves of candy, mints, and gum. We tend to ignore those things because we're not huge fans of A) loading our children up with sugar, and B) encouraging spontaneous buying on useless things (I'm actually a huge fan of spontaneous buying on valuable things... lol).

As we're standing there, she kind of glances over and looks up at the candy.

She's calculating.

She knows that if she asks me straight out, the answer is no. So, instead, she reaches over and grabs my hand and looks up at me. "I love you, Daddy," she said with a sweet smile. And then didn't say anything else for a minute.

The next person in line leaves, we take another step forward. Then she looks up at me again and says, "Thanks for taking me to the store, Daddy. I love spending time with you."

My marketing brain knows I'm getting conned bad right now. But the emotion of it is very real. My daughter, the eyes... I mean, ahh! I just can't resist. I'm chuckling inside even as I'm being ruthlessly influenced by this cute little girl.

Finally, she pops the question. "Daddy, I wonder... can we buy some gum? Not the sugary kind that hurts your teeth, but you know... the kind with xylitol. Mommy says that kind is good for your teeth. I really like the pink one. Can we buy that one? Please?"

I looked down at my beautiful girl and knew she had got me. The person at the cash register was looking at me with this expression that said, "Oh, boy... you already lost this game, dude."

Sure enough, I reached over, grabbed the xylitol bubble gum, and stuck it on the cart. Mary got all excited, and I gave her a big hug, and I was happy to do it for her.

What did my daughter do here?

In short, she knew me so well that she could push all the buttons that moved me to action.

I'm going to give you some insights on how to structure your copy so that it will have higher persuasive pulling power... but you need to do the work (if you haven't already) to come to really understand your ideal buyer.

Do you remember our discussion on RAS Triggers – that section of our brain that forces us to pay attention to things that are important to us?

Your mission is to understand your ideal buyer so well that you can activate their RAS Triggers... and hold their attention by giving them solutions to their challenges and helping them fulfill their desires.

Let me give you an example of how this works in your messaging...

Attracting the Beekeepers

I was sitting in Perry Marshall's small home office on the second floor of his Berwin, IL home. Perry Marshall is one of the world's leading experts in Google Ad Words, Facebook Ads, and is challenging the medical field with his ideas on evolution and cancer treatments. He's a brilliant man and author of several books, including *Evolution 2.0* and *The 80/20 Of Sales and Marketing*.

The chairs were arranged in a semi-circle around Perry's desk. Around the room sat three other men. All of us were there for a two-day private hands-on private consultation with Perry.

On the second day, during one of the breaks, we spent some time getting to know each other better.

"I just finished building out my fifth beehive," I mentioned.

The man across from me smiled, "That's great. I have bees as well."

"Really?" the other man replied. "So do I!"

The three of us turned to the fourth man with a questioning look.

He gave us a funny grin, "I just sold my hives and equipment about two months ago because we moved."

I was amazed. What are the odds that four men, from different parts of the world, running totally different businesses, should all be beekeepers and be gathered in Perry's home office?

We started asking about other hobbies and activities, and quickly found out that the similarities between us were far more than our differences. SCUBA diving, large families, blue as a favorite color, love of travel, etc.

When Perry came back, we laughingly told him all about it. I thought he would be surprised.

But he wasn't.

"Yeah," he said. "I already knew most of that. I used all that to target you guys and get you to come here."

I was shocked.

Perry went on, "The best marketing is a one-on-one conversation with another human being. I realized that my ideal client tends to have specific, sometimes quirky hobbies and interests. So, I crafted my marketing for these two-day intensives to call out you guys. And it worked—obviously."

Perry used ideas, words, and images in his marketing that he knew would fire up our RAS Triggers.

Improve Your Copy, Improve Your Response Rates

As I said, the most important thing you can do to improve the response rates on the Opt-In Page is to write very persuasive, compelling copy. Nothing else will move the needle more than this.

Over the years, one of my companies has trained more than 30,000 copywriters. There are many techniques to writing effective, persuasive copy, but few things make a bigger impact for minimal effort than using the S.A.U.C.E method we developed.

Here is a summary of the method. For more details, you can also refer to the training model we included in your bonus materials.

Before I share the S.A.U.C.E method with you, you might be asking yourself...

"Why do I need to learn how to write effective, persuasive copy? Can't I just hire a copywriter to do it for me?"

Yes, of course you can hire a copywriter (and we can recommend a few highly qualified, certified writers to you).

But the reality is, everything you write should be persuasive. You want people to take action so they can get solutions to their challenges and fulfill their deepest desires, right?

Yes! So, your writing—emails, reports, video scripts, etc.—needs to be as effective and persuasive as possible. The S.A.U.C.E method will help do that.

The other reason you should learn effective copywriting techniques is so that you can spot a quality, persuasive copywriter when you do hire one. There are tens of thousands of copywriters out there and there are very few really qualified, high-pulling writers. You need one that will deliver results.

Writers that understand the principles in the S.A.U.C.E method will be far more effective than those that do not. It's that simple.

So, here's the method summary for you...

S.A.U.C.E is an acronym. Here is what each letter means and how you can effectively use it.

S = Specific to Your Audience.

Use jargon and language that is dripping with things important to them.

Invoke the "Power of One" by focusing on one major benefit or solution. Stay focused!

A = Actionable.

What action do you want them to take when they are done reading your ad, article, or message?

Make sure you have a clearly defined "Trust Journey" (see details in this chapter). This will help create each step of your funnel and ensure that your messaging is on point at each step.

U = Urgent

Give them a reason to take action RIGHT NOW!

What is the deadline? Limited space? The price goes up if they wait?

Clearly define why your offer is urgent.

Urgency is one of the most powerful ways to get people to take action. But how do you create urgency?

All humans have three core, fundamental needs. These are:

- **Safety** – We all need to feel safe... specifically, that means we need to know that we can stay alive and be relatively free from major physical, emotional, or mental injury.
- **Growth** – All humans need to grow, moving from where they are at right now to a higher place... more education, better health, stronger relationships, deeper love, fancier stuff, etc.
- **Belonging** – We are social creatures. We need to belong to something bigger than ourselves and have emotional connections to other humans.

We feel a sense of urgency to act when any of those three areas are in jeopardy. If you're in a movie theater and the fire alarm goes off, then you smell smoke and see other people freaking out, it's highly likely you'll get moving!

We also feel a sense of urgency when one of these three areas stands to benefit. When I was dating my wife, Margie, she said to me, "There's a church devotional tomorrow night. I'm going. Are you going? If you are, I'd love a ride." She said it with a smile that could melt the North

Pole and eyes that could light up the universe. So, YES! I was going, and YES! I could pick her up!

C = Clear

Clear is the opposite of confusing. State your offer, benefits, message, and ideas as simply and clearly as possible.

A very easy way to gauge this is using a Flesch-Kincaid Score (FK Score). This is a score that helps determine readability based on grade levels.

The lower the score, the easier it is to read.

As a general rule of thumb, I will only release my writing if the FK Score is under 7.

You can find FK Score calculators online. I've used www.Readable.io for over 10 years. It is very simple and accurate. Find one you like and run all your copy through it.

You might ask why I set my standard at FK Score 7. The answer is very simple. I've tested thousands of pieces of copy. A lower FK score consistently performs better, pulling more sales and getting better results.

Every serious marketer and A-Level copywriter I know agrees on this point. It is a massive high-leverage point that is very easy to implement, but often overlooked.

(As a reference, this book averages an FK Score of 6.)

E = Emotional

All human beings make decisions based on emotion – it's the way we are programmed.

That's because emotions drive desires and desires drive actions.

There are eight key persuasion desires. These desires move people to action faster than all the others. Here is a quick summary of these desires:

The Top 8 Persuasive Desires

1. **Significance** – This is the number one driver to purchase. All human beings have a need to be respected and seen as unique and valuable. As you'll see, the other 7 Desires essentially stem from the desire to be respected and feel significant.

2. **Intimacy** – Emotional and physical intimacy show us that we are good enough for another human being to devote themselves to us. We have enough value to have another person give us their time, their love, their secrets, and their life.

3. **Personal Growth** – As human beings, we have two abilities that no other creature has... the ability to self-analyze and the ability to imagine. These two attributes compel us to want more and become better. And, as a benefit, when we do, the world praises us and validates our significance.

4. **Health** – Our physical bodies house our soul or our mind or our essence or whatever you choose to call it. Our physical body is not who we are. It is the vehicles transporting us through life. Because of this, we hunger to keep it running smoothly. Our physical sensations and functionality define our feelings and create our opportunities in life. As they say, "If you don't have your health, you don't have anything!"

5. **Prosperity** – This includes financial wealth, but also success and security in all the other categories of our life. The desire to prosper drives athletes, business owners, politicians, parents, and all of humanity. And, it helps that prosperity is rewarded with social accolades!

6. **Joy** – It has been said that people exist "that they may have joy". I totally agree! Life is meant to be filled with joy and happiness and laughter. Of course, it doesn't always turn out that way. Each of us go through seasons, but we look forward to better days of joy.

7. **Fear** – Before you say, "We don't want fear! How is that a persuasive Desire?!", consider how profitable horror movies,

haunted houses, roller coasters, and other scary, thrilling experiences have been through all ages of time. Fear gives us contrast in life. It gives weight and meaning to joy, intimacy, respect, and health. It teaches us what works and what does not work. Yes, as strange as it sounds, we desire fear.

8. **Scarcity** – As a symbol of our uniqueness and individuality, we seek for things that others don't have. This can include a special deal that others missed out on, a rare gem or metal, stuff reserved for a certain class of people, experiences that can only be had in one place or at one time.

As you review your copy, analyze it to see if it is full of the emotions that drive these desires. If it isn't, you can instantly boost response rates by adding these elements to your message.

Always keep the buyer in mind. If they desire to be wealthy, spending a great deal of time focusing on becoming healthier will not give you a higher response rate. Stay congruent with what they want and the problems they are trying to solve.

7 – Create the "Thank You" Page

The "Thank You" Page is the page you send them to directly after they register for the Free Offer.

A version of the "Thank You" Page will be used at the end of Phase Two after they have finalized all their purchases with you, including seeing the In-Cart Bump Offer and the One-Time Offer.

Your CRM will have "Thank You" Page templates that can help this be very simple and easy.

The "Thank You" Page is very simple and includes these elements and copy:

- **Headline** – This is a congratulations note affirming that they have made a great decision. Be sure to mention the name of the Free Offer so that they know they are in the right place.
- **Image or Graphic** – Include an image of yourself (or the expert/guru if that's not you) and/or a box shot of the Free Offer they just registered for. There are a number of graphic programs that can help you create professional product images and box shots. However, to keep things simple, just use Canva (www.Canva.com). The free version will do fine for you.
- **Access Information** – Tell them how they can access their Free Offer. Typically, you'll send them an email with an access link and password information. Something simple like… "An email is on its way to you right now with full access info" is good enough.
- **Call to Action** – In the future, you'll invite them to go deeper into your funnel (more on that later), but for now, just invite them to engage in your world. This could be an invite for them to follow you on social media, read an article, listen to your podcast, or send you an email with feedback/a testimonial. Simply put it at the end under a sub-header that reads, "Here's the Next Step…"

8 – Write the Welcome and Deliverables Email

As soon as they register for the Free Offer, they need to get two emails from you:

- **A Welcome email** – This is an email that congratulates them, embraces them as a new member of your digital family, and helps them connect with you emotionally.

- **A Deliverables Email** – This email is very simple, short, and sweet. It includes all the access information they need to get the Free Offer.

The Welcome Email

Here is a template for the Welcome Email copy and structure (when I do templates, I put the variable stuff in brackets and all caps [JUST LIKE THIS!] to make it easy on you!)...

- Subject Line – "[NAME], welcome to [COMPANY NAME]
- Salutation – Hi [Name]!
- Welcome Note – Welcome them to your digital family, company, or however you want to phrase it. This is their first personal communication from you, so make it personal and genuine.
- Your Origin Story – Tell them why you created the solution and give the backstory. Be sure to be vulnerable, real, and sincere. Should be 1-5 short paragraphs.
- Success Stories – Tell them a quick success story or two from people that have used your system or that you've helped. Include your feelings on their success and your passion for helping others. Should be 1-5 short paragraphs.
- Benefits Statement – Give them an outline of some of the benefits they'll receive by being part of your digital family. Should be 3-7 bullet points.
- Call to Action – Always invite people on your list to take action. In this email, you want to encourage them to do at least two things:
    - Connect with you on social media. Since you're running Facebook Ads, it is best to invite them to engage with you on FB. This will help your Quality Scores.

- Consume the Free Offer. Give them some quick insights on your favorite part of the Free Offer and some insider tips/tricks that you didn't share with them yet. This little bit of extra value goes a very long way.
- Close: Give them a warm closing statement and your name.
- Postscript (The ol' PS): Tell them how to contact you if they have any questions or concerns. Let them know you are available.

This email can be longer – between 500 and 1500 words. They want to know more about you and this is the best time to tell them.

You should send it immediately after they register for the Free Offer.

The Deliverables Email

The Deliverables Email can include the following elements and copy… and you should know that your CRM likely already has a cookie-cutter template for this that will include their access information to the Free Offer.

- Subject Line: [NAME] access [FREE OFFER NAME] inside. Keep this handy!
- Salutation: Hello [NAME]
- Congratulations: Restate and reaffirm what a great choice they made by getting the Free Offer.
- Benefits List: Give them 3-5 very short bullet points on the benefits they'll receive. This can be the exact same list you used on the Opt-In Page. Repetition is great right here.
- Access Information: Give them their username and password. If this is a universal username and password that they will use for all future products, then be sure to mention that. It's a huge benefit to them to not have to remember lots of passwords to access your solutions.

- Close: Give them a warm closing statement and your name.

That's it. This whole thing should be less than 300 words. Shorter is better.

Like with the Welcome Email, you should send it immediately after they register for the Free Offer. Both emails should arrive within seconds or minutes of each other.

Setting Up Automated Emails in Your CRM

All decent CRMs for funnel building, like Kartra or ClickFunnels, have automations that can trigger email sequences. For a detailed over-the-shoulder workshop of how to set up your emails in Kartra, you can visit www.Strahes.com/funnel-setup.

Summary

In 2018, I decided to expand one of my companies, Copywriter Marketer. I needed to do it without a great deal of overheads and wanted a rapid turnaround of cash flow.

Most experts that I talked to said that I could hope for a 90-120 day return on ad spend, which was totally unacceptable to me. I knew from working with hundreds of other companies that when you have the right offer stack, you can turn cash flow in 30 days… or in some cases, much faster.

The key was to create a Free Offer that did two things:

Had a very high conversion rate—in excess of 40%.

AND

Gave incredible value while simultaneously preparing the ideal customer to buy more, both immediately and long term. (This is a process that I call "Salting the Oats", which we discussed in detail in the introduction to Phase One.)

I walked through the process and ideas that I've shared with you in this chapter. The result was the creation of a Free Offer called "10 Predictors of Success as a Freelance Copywriter". Within the first six months, that one Free Offer attracted more than 19,570 new subscribers and generated more than $250,000 in sales.

The best part is that our return on ad spend turnaround time was less than 72 hours. Our average cost to acquire a customer was around $47 and our Initial Customer Value (the value of the customer after they go through the initial sales funnel sequence that you're building with the help of this book) was $72... or an average profit per buyer of $35 in less than a week.

Those numbers remained consistent for many years without changing a single word or image in the Free Offer or the ads we used to drive traffic to them.

The Free Offer is not the only player in that scene, but it is the first step, the first opportunity for your ideal buyer to begin to trust you and emotionally connect with you.

Make it the best you can... not perfect... but excellent and good enough.

Action Checklist

Here's your step-by-step action plan for building out your Free Offer.

Identify the "Bleeding Neck" – This is where you do the research to understand your ideal buyer intimately. Don't guess on this. You need to figure out something that is super urgent to them right now. This should be a problem they need to solve or a benefit they really want.

Create an Information Product – Follow the steps below to create something free that instantly gives them a solution to their problem.

- ☐ **1 – Define the Deliverable** – As I stated before, the most important thing you can do is identify the urgent challenge they need solved or desire they want fulfilled.
- ☐ **2 – Choose the Format** – Different formats that are commonly used are Cheat Sheets, Written Report or Guide, Video Mini-Course, Audio Mini-Course, and others. I strongly recommend that your Free Offer format is a Cheat Sheet or a Written Report of some kind.
- ☐ **3 – Create the Free Offer** – Set up a non-negotiable time to get this done. Just do it.
- ☐ **4 – Format and Shine It Up** – How involved this process is will depend on your audience. You might need to get a professional editor... or you might just bang something out and go with it. The key is to know your audience well enough that you have a good idea of what they will resonate with.
- ☐ **5 – Set Up Your Free Offer in CRM** – Obviously, the step-by-step process will depend on your CRM. The goal here is to get your Free Offer to your customer automatically when they fill out an opt-in form.
- ☐ **6 – Create the Opt-In Form and Page** – Create a form where they can submit their name and phone number. Then, make a page to put the form on. Your CRM should have a template for this. See pages ## through ## for details.
- ☐ **7 – Create the "Thank You" Page** – The "Thank You" Page is the page you send them to directly after they register for the Free Offer. Your CRM will have "Thank You" Page templates that can help this be very simple and easy. See page ## through ## for details.

☐ **8 – Write the Welcome and Deliverable Emails –** As soon as they register for the Free Offer, they need to get two emails from you: A Welcome email and a Deliverables Email. See page ## through ## for details.

CHAPTER 4

Paid Ad Secrets That Pay

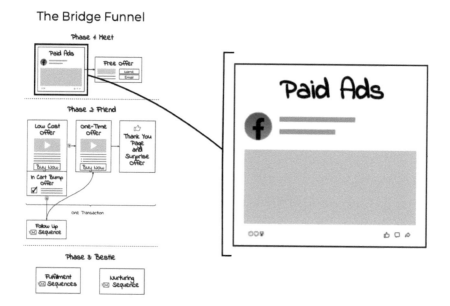

His voice was frantic. In fact, I'm sure he was—or had been—crying.

"Joshua", Edward said. "I don't know what happened, but Google is telling me I owe them $12,000 for the ads I ran last week. And Facebook wants another $7,000. What did I do wrong? How am I going to pay that?"

A few weeks before, Edward (name changed... I like doing that to protect my friends!), a friend from Church, had approached me about an online business idea he had. He and his wife made unique jewelry that a number of us had commented on and admired.

"Joshua," he said to me. "I think we can sell our jewelry and run some training videos on how we do it. You know, teach people our techniques. I think people would buy both. What do you think?"

"Well, there are certainly other people successfully doing the same thing. I'm not an expert in that niche, but I think you could make a go at it."

"Great! We already built a website. I've been working on that for a couple of months. I'm going to run some ads on Google and Facebook."

I put on the most earnest and serious face I could muster. "Kevin, listen to me. It is not overly complicated to run ads, but you do need to know a few key things so that you don't lose your shirt. I've seen people blow tens of thousands of dollars in a few days. I don't think you have that kind of money to waste. Before you run those ads, let me sit down with you and walk you through it."

He nodded, smiled, and said he would.

And then he didn't.

And now, he was in the hole by almost $20,000 with nothing to show for it. I think he picked up 10 or 15 customers, netting him about $500.

I wish I could tell you that Edward is an exception—an idiot outlier that lost his shirt to stupidity tax. But sadly, he's not.

Major companies and small companies alike spend ad money and never see a return, or even worse, are not sure if they have seen a return on their ad spend.

During my first consultation session with Corel, a major international software company, I asked them to show me how much they were spending on ads. I asked them to give me a list of the specific customers that came from those ads. I also wanted to know who had spent how much and when.

"We don't really have that kind of data," was the reply.

I've heard something similar from dozens of companies through the years. Financial advisors, newsletters, universities, software, hardware, non-profits, etc.

Very few companies really know what their return on ad spend is and how fast they are getting it. I've discovered that when you don't know, you're definitely losing money, or, at the least, you're not maximizing your ad spend.

I love this quote from Thomas S. Monson:

> "When performance is measured, performance improves. When performance is measured and reported, the rate of improvement accelerates"

You need an air-tight tracking system so that you know exactly how your ads are performing. This allows you to optimize your systems and maximize your profits.

The good news is that with the CRM and other systems you're building with the help of this book, most of the tracking will happen automatically.

Why spend money on ads?

When dealing with startup companies—especially influencers and small entrepreneurs—I get asked this question:

"Why do I have to spend money on ads? Can't I just do content marketing and SEO and get people to come to me that way? It's free and will save me money."

Earlier, we discussed the pros and cons of content marketing.

Again, the simple answer is you need rapid, consistent results. And to get that, you need paid ads.

And, again, eventually, you will use a combination of paid ads and content marketing. But first, get your ads and your Optimal Selling

Strategy in place. These are the things that will help you get profits in the door quickly.

Here are a few more reasons why you should focus on paid ads right now, at this stage of the game...

First, content marketing takes time.

Facebook, LinkedIn, Google, and the other platforms love content and will reward you handsomely... eventually.

I teach freelance copywriter students that they need to create "Daily Compelling Content". They should post great content 5-7 times a day for 3-6 months before they can expect to see results.

After working with over 30,000 copywriters, I've found that very few have the discipline to do that... and each day you miss, the gods of social media penalize you and reduce your traffic.

Paid ads run automatically for you. They don't sleep. They don't forget. They just run and run and run until you turn them off.

Second, the platforms control distribution, you don't.

I currently have around 15,000 connections on LinkedIn. When I publish content, I rejoice when over 900 people actually see it. LinkedIn is NOT sharing my content with all of my connections and followers. In fact, only a fraction of the people see it. It's the same with Facebook, Instagram, Twitter, etc.

The social media engines are designed to maximize their profits, not yours, especially when it comes to content.

With paid ads, you get to control who, how many, and where your ads are displayed.

Marketing is a numbers game, no matter how you look at it. I can turn a paid ad on, and within an hour, have thousands or even tens of thousands of people see my message.

It takes a long time to build up a list and a following—sometimes years.

Third, you and I are not as smart as the AI systems.

When you only do content marketing, you need to think carefully about where you place your content. You can have the best content in the world, but if the right people don't see it, your message is invisible or wasted.

Google and Facebook have invested billions of dollars into creating Artificial Intelligence systems that magically match your message with the right people. They can optimize very minutely, focusing on people who will click, who might buy, who will engage, and other parameters. It's incredible and the results are magical and profitable for the marketers that know how to use their system.

You simply can't have that kind of reach or have that kind of data-crunching by yourself.

Paid ads give you instant access to the right people and instant results. I can turn ads on in the morning and have paying customers within minutes.

I can spend $30-$50 to test new messages and offers and know within 3-5 days what the winning message is. Over time, the AI system gathers data and increases the effectiveness of my ads.

With all that being said, running paid ads can also be a very dangerous proposition... like it was for Edward.

This chapter is not meant to be a comprehensive treatise on paid ads. There are entire courses on the subject. But, in reality, you don't need a PhD in Facebook or Google to win at paid ads.

Here are the key things you need to do to begin successfully running paid ads on Facebook. We will focus on Facebook because it is the easiest to learn, the fastest to deploy with the fewest pitfalls, and will give you access to all the customers you need to get started.

There are 10 major steps to safely and successfully run Facebook Ads. Let's go through each of them now...

1 – Confirm Your Identity with Facebook

If you have not already done this, do it now. This will reduce the chances of your account getting blocked or ads being banned.

You'll hear me say that a lot… "This will help you not be banned". The reason is that Facebook really likes to ban small advertisers. This can be costly, frustrating, and time-consuming. You want to avoid this as much as possible. (More on this point way down at Step #9: How to Avoid Being Banned on Facebook and How to Get Unbanned!)

To confirm your identity with Facebook, you simply upload a valid photo ID. The fastest way to do all of this is to Google "Confirm ID with Facebook". It will take you directly to the page where you can do that.

Pro-Tip… You might have to do this several times. Most of my clients do this with their personal accounts, their business accounts, AND their Business Manager accounts… and if Facebook detects any "unusual" activity, they'll ask you to do it yet again.

Most of the time, you simply upload the ID again and you're fine. Occasionally, especially with Business Manager Accounts, they like to talk to you live on the phone.

This should take you no more than 30 minutes to complete and is free.

2 – Create Facebook Business Page

If you don't already have a Facebook Page for your business, take the time to create one now. Jump through all the hoops and give them as much information as you can. Add a description, address, cover photo, profile picture, etc.

The more information you can add, the more "legit" they will think you are. Plus, the AI will use this information to help match your ads with the right person. In other words, you're helping improve your response rates.

Once you have the page fully set up, immediately make 5-10 posts. Again, you're both validating that you're a real business and giving the AI fodder to know who your ideal buyer is.

And yes, this all helps you to not get banned!

This is because the more content and interactions you have on your Page, the better your overall Account Score will be. Facebook will clock down or shut down accounts with low Account Scores. Don't worry about it too much... just post quality content, engage with real followers and buyers, and be a legit business.

After the initial posts, plan on posting another 3-7 times a week. If anyone comments on the post, take a minute to reply. Facebook's AI looks at all of this.

It should go without saying that your content should be relevant and interesting to your ideal buyer.

A few years ago, one of my small business clients was having a hard time getting their ads to convert. Traffic was low, clicks were low, and purchases were low.

"Kim," I said. "Have you been consistently posting content?"

"Yes! Actually, I post a few times every day."

"That's great. Let's look at what you're posting."

Kim owned a business training yoga and Pilates instructors on building and managing their business, both as part of a larger gym and as independent shops.

When I reviewed both her Facebook and LinkedIn accounts, I instantly knew the problem.

Just about every post had to do with animals... mostly cats... with a number of different kinds of rescue animals, humane society causes, etc.

Keep your content relevant and useful to your ideal buyer.

We've included a short guide on effective content in your bonus materials.

I want to stress that this is NOT about content marketing. The only reasons to create content at this stage of the game is to keep Facebook happy so you can run ads.

3 – Set Up a Meta Business Suite

This is a very simple step to complete. Be sure you're logged into Facebook / Meta and go to www.business.facebook.com. You'll be prompted to set up a Meta Business Manager if you don't already have one.

> **NOTE:** You can run ads from your personal Ads Center. I know, it can be confusing… you have a personal Ads Center that allows you to run ads directly from your personal account… AND you have an Ads Manager in your Business Suite.
>
> The data does not cross over between the two. Think of them as two different universes.
>
> In the long term, it is much better for you to run and manage ads from the Ads Manager on the business side of Facebook/Metaverse.

This should take you less than an hour to complete.

4 – Set Up and Install a Meta Pixel

A Meta Pixel is a tiny bit of code that Meta uses to track… everything.

The more ads you run, the more visitors to your website and Opt-In Pages, the more content you post, the better "trained" your pixel will be.

A well "trained" pixel will help you increase conversion rates and reduce ad-spend rates. This has a huge impact on your return on ad spend (ROAS) and lifetime customer value.

Setting up a pixel is easy. Installing it on your website and Opt-In Pages is a little more technical. Facebook has some simple tutorials to help you.

To set up your pixel, go to your Meta Business Manager. Select Business Settings, and then go to the Data Sources section. Select Pixels and follow the prompts to add a pixel.

Installing a pixel on your website can be tricky depending on what platform you're using. If you use WordPress and Divi, you simply grab the Pixel code from Facebook and paste it into the integrations box. Done.

Other websites can be more or less complicated. One of the best options here is to outsource this. It just needs to be done and it is very simple for someone with a bit of tech skills. Our team can help you set up your pixel and make sure it is working properly. Contact us at contact@strahes.com for more information.

> Pro-tip... be sure to give your pixel a name that makes sense to you. Over time, you might have several pages and several pixels. Be sure that the name you give it right now will make sense in the future, not only to you... but to anyone you might hire down the road.

5 – Set up Server-Side Tracking

When Apple changed their tracking and data policies, it destroyed much of the traditional buyer tracking methods and technologies.

To get around this, Facebook created what they call "Server-Side Tracking", or sometimes called "Conversion API". Essentially, instead of Facebook relying on website-based cookies and user permissions to track behavior such as purchases, they include a code that runs traffic through your server where the data is collected.

(Side note: It is interesting to me that a law and policy that was supposed to make your online actions more private forced the industry to get creative and develop new technology that honors the law/policy and improves online behavior tracking. This is a testament to me of human ingenuity and resilience. Remember that you have the same ability to face obstacles and overcome them.)

You will need access to the server that hosts your website if you're going to do this yourself. If you do not have some decent tech skills, I recommend outsourcing this as well.

This should take no more than 30 minutes to get done... unless you need to learn the ins-and-outs of the code side of a website... then it will take you around three hours.

6 – Write Copy for Your Ads

Copy is king... meaning, the words you use will have the highest impact on your conversion rates.

Remember, focus on ONE benefit and keep all the supporting reasons why and feature sets focused on that one benefit.

When I was a relatively new copywriter, I had the opportunity to work on a project with Mark Ford. Mark Ford has built several $100 million-plus businesses and is one of the best copywriters in the world.

I was writing a long-copy sales letter for a new financial newsletter he was starting—the Palm Beach Letter. I worked for weeks to get a headline and lead just right.

My palms were practically raining sweat and my heart was pounding like a blacksmith's hammer when I sat down in his office for my "peer review" session.

"Hi, Joshua, let's see what you've got," he said.

I slid the letter across his massive mahogany desk and sat bolt upright waiting for his reaction.

He looked up 30 seconds later and said, "This will never work. You have to rework it."

To be honest, I was shattered. I really wanted to impress him and I really wanted this project to have explosive success. It would open so many doors for me.

"Umm. Ok," I said. "What needs to be fixed on it?"

"The headline and lead are a tossed salad. You've got at least four main benefits in here and then you touch on another three in the lead."

Taking out a red pen, he began circling different phrases to illustrate his point.

"Joshua, you need to focus on ONE thing. One big idea."

Despite my nervousness, I wanted to defend my work.

"Well, don't we offer all those benefits with the newsletter? I wanted to show them all the great stuff they will get."

"Yeah, we do. But, you'll confuse them with all this stuff… and a confused mind never buys. Just pick one of these and focus on it."

And that is what I did. And yes, the letter was a smashing success.

Your ad needs to focus on one main idea and benefit. Yes, I know you can do a million great things for them. For now, pick the one that you believe is most beneficial and desirable to your ideal buyer.

To publish your ads, you will use a feature Facebook has called, "Dynamic Ads". You feed the Facebook engine five versions of three main sections of your ad, plus nine images. Then, using their multi-billion dollar AI engine, Facebook mixes and matches the copy of your ad and the images to create new ads on the fly, optimized for each individual viewer.

It is incredible technology and very effective—especially when you're just starting out. The same copy principles we discussed in

Chapter 3 apply here. Now is a good time to go back and review those as you prepare to write your ads.

The three main areas you will write copy for are:

- Primary Text
- Description Text
- Headline Text

Let's take a look at each one.

Primary Text

This is the main copy you see on a Facebook Ad. It sits above the image.

Facebook will show 125 characters in the Primary Text field and then truncate the rest behind a "show more" link. (This paragraph, including this note, is 171 characters.)

There is a debate about short versus long copy. Meaning, should you write a relatively long Primary Text… or keep it short?

The answer is … it depends on your audience and their awareness level.

You can use these standards as a simple guide:

- Highly aware of their challenge and desire = Short Length Copy
- Highly familiar with you and your solution = Short Length Copy
- Less aware of their challenge and desire = Medium Length Copy
- Less aware of you and your solution = Medium Length Copy
- Unaware of their challenge and desire = Long Length Copy

- Unaware of you and your solution = Long Length Copy

For simplicity, here's how I'll define short, medium, and long copy in the context of Facebook Ads. Emails, sales letters, and video scripts have different definitions...

- Short copy = 30 words or less
- Medium copy = 100 words or less
- Long copy = over 100 words (and can be more... one of our clients ran a very successful ad for more than two years that was just shy of 400 words.)

The key is to keep it tight. Only use as many words as are necessary to get them to take action.

Now, here's the good news...

Because of how Dynamic Ads work, the best idea is to try all three versions—short, medium, and long. Facebook will optimize for the one that works best. You will write five versions of your Primary Text, so I recommend you do the following:

- Two short versions
- Two medium versions
- One long version

If you know for sure that the awareness level is extremely low, you would simply flip that—two long, two medium, and one short.

Over time, you can test this more, but this is the best way to begin.

One of our clients hosts free ESL (English as a second language) classes. Here are Primary Text examples:

Short Version:

Do you struggle with English?

Our Free ESL classes can help you learn English fast—just 8 weeks!

Everything's included... all the materials, plus a private tutor! All FREE.

Register today! (31 words... 86 characters.)

Medium Version:

New! ESL classes are now open... at no cost to you!

Yes, ESL classes are now available in your area. Gain confidence in English. Shop, bank, and meet new people without embarrassment.

Yes! You can transform your life quickly by learning English. Master everyday English in under 8 weeks with our unique teaching systems... all for FREE.

All class materials are included. Small, private class sizes—less than 12 students! Register today!   (74 words... 434 Characters.)

Long Version

Faith-based ESL Classes—FREE

Discover the power of learning English, not just using your mind, but also your heart and soul. In our FREE ESL classes, we invite you to partner with God and ask for His help to help you learn faster and bless your life more fully.

This is unlike any other ESL class available anywhere. Our system is proven by over 1 million students worldwide. Yes, it is free—no cost to you—because of generous donations from God-fearing people who want to serve others with the gift of free ESL classes.

Our ESL classes are small—usually less than 20 students. We provide all the materials, a private setting to help you learn faster, tutors to help you pronounce words right and get social situations right, and faith-based teaching methods that will help you feel God's love and power.

Yes, you can learn English. Yes, we have a fast-track program so that you can learn conversational English in 6 weeks or less. Yes, it is free to you. Yes, this will bless your life.

Come join us. Because class sizes are small, space is limited, so register today. (192 words... 1098 characters.)

Here's a pro-tip for your Primary Text... You can use little icons in your copy to catch attention. Graphical images of checkboxes ✅, emojis 😀 🙈, and other small elements 🎉 💯. Don't use too many or Facebook will reject your ad, but a few can be very helpful when used appropriately.

Headline Text

This is a tight, benefit-laced call to action.
You get about 40 characters here before Facebook cuts it off. That's not a lot.
An ESL class headline we've used successfully for several years is:

FREE ESL classes are now open! Register today! (46 characters.)

As with your Primary Text, you'll write five versions of this. Follow the same process of two short versions, two medium versions, and one long version. In this case, short is under 40 characters (not words... characters), medium is 60 characters, and long is 100 characters.

Here's a medium version:

> FREE ESL classes are now open! We can help. Register today! (59 characters.)

And a long version:

> Do you struggle with English? FREE ESL classes are now open! Learn basic English in 12 weeks or less. Register today! (118 characters.)

Again, with Dynamic Ads, Facebook will automatically optimize for the Headline Text that performs the best.

Description Text

The Description Text shows up under the Headline Text, but only on certain formats. Remember, Facebook will display your ad in a lot of different places, including within the Instagram network, chat, stories, and other places.

There is not always space for the Description Text, but it plays an important role when there is room, like in the standard Facebook feed.

You will write five versions of this description. The best way to think of this is a postscript summary with a bonus. Have you ever read a letter, and at the end, there is a postscript that summarizes the big idea and promise of the promotion... and then adds a lovely, juicy little benefit at the end?

For example, one year, I did a year-end summit where I interviewed 20 top influencers and asked them what ONE THING they were going to do to create success in the coming year.

One of the speakers, Rha Goddess, offered an amazing bonus. In one of my emails, I dropped this little bombshell...

> P.S. Would you like some help discovering your Purpose?
>
> During the Summit, one of the speakers, Rha Goddess, gave us FREE access to her amazing course called "The Evangelical Model".
>
> This course is designed to help you find your purpose. If you missed the Summit, you can still get recordings... and FREE access to Rha's course. (A $197 value!)
>
> Rha is a world leader in helping people find and live their calling and purpose in life. This is a rare opportunity to get help with one of the most important questions of your life.
>
> You can get her entire course... FREE... just for being part of The One Thing Changed Summit. Register today!

See how that feels? Your description copy should carry the same feeling. Give them a gift that they'll love... and one that will help them want to be part of your world.

Your Description Text should include the following elements:

- One Benefit – Reminder of the key benefit
- Surprise bonus – Benefit of some kind that you didn't mention before
- Urgency – A reason for them to act right away
- Call to Action – Tell them exactly what to do next

Here's a long-copy example from our ESL ads:

> Yes! Our ESL classes are totally FREE because of generous private donors. You'll get everything you need, including private tutors, at no cost to you. Learn English FAST with our unique system. Register today. Space is limited! (228 characters.)

Facebook will truncate the Description text and, in some cases, only display 25 characters—very short. But, again, copy length is dependent on your ideal buyer's awareness level.

Here's a medium version of the description:

> Free ESL with private tutors! Limited Seats. Register Now. (58 characters.)

And finally, a short version:

> Free ESL tutor. Join Now! (25 characters.)

The copy for your ads deserves your best attention and thinking. You should plan on spending no more than 10 hours on this, including research and revisions.

7 – Find and Edit Images for Your Ads

Best Practices for Images

You will upload nine images for your Dynamic Ad set. Here are a few best practices for your images:

- Included people... usually a single person that is relatable to your ideal buyer's demographics. Be sure they can see the eyes of the person in the image.
- You can use artwork, cartoon-style graphics, or things like charts... but be careful not to have a bunch of text as I'll explain below.
- The person in the image should show the benefit you're promising.
- Use high-contrast resolution. This helps your image stand out.
- Include one or two black and white images. These tend to really stand out and perform well.
- Minimal to zero text. If you do have text, it cannot be more than 20% of your image or Facebook will reject it. Also, the text must be relevant. You cannot include any kinds of arrows, buttons, or graphics... just text. Text must be clear to read.
- Landscape images work best. Facebook will crop them as needed for the different formats. You can preview the different formats when you upload the image to make sure it will work.
- If you don't have original images or pictures, you have a few options for obtaining or creating them.
- Your Smartphone – Start taking pictures of stuff and people that relate to your business. Original images perform very well. If you take a picture of someone, be sure to get their permission and fee waiver to use it in an ad.
- Royalty-Free Photos – You can find royalty-free images at sites like www.Unsplash.com, https://burst.shopify.com/, or https://www.pexels.com/.
- Stock Photos – Sites like www.ShutterStock.com or www.IStockPhoto.com have images you can buy.

- Graphic Design Sites – Sites like www.Canva.com and www.Ripl.com are relatively inexpensive and can help you create thousands of different designs and graphics.

This should take you no more than two hours to find and upload your images. Keep it simple.

8 – Build Your Campaign in the Facebook AdCenter

You now have all the elements you need to actually build your ad. I'll outline a few key points to pay attention to.

A word of warning… there are thousands of settings and ways to set up Facebook Ads. It can be very confusing and frustrating. The key here is to keep it simple. Right now, only a few things really matter.

We will focus on those key things.

If you are not familiar with all the technical aspects of setting up a Facebook Ad, we created a detailed guide for you, "How to Set Up Profitable Facebook Ads for Beginners". It goes through every screen and setting so you can get it done quickly and get it done right the first time.

You can find the guide in your bonus materials.

For now, here are the key points you need to pay close attention to. These settings will help you avoid paying Facebook without getting results.

I'll give you the name of the section in Facebook and the key action to take to make your ads effective. The best way to use this section… and the free, detailed guide… is to review it while you're at your computer actually putting your ads together.

- Campaign Type – Select TRAFFIC. You will use your Facebook Ads to drive traffic to your landing page.

- A/B Test – Make sure this is UNCHECKED. If it is checked, you won't be able to run Dynamic Ads. Split testing is very powerful but adds too much complexity at this point. Stick to Dynamic Ads for now.
- Advanced Campaign Budget – Make sure this is UNCHECKED. It is useful if you are running multiple AdSets with complex and diverse objectives. Right now, you just want to keep it simple and make some money, right? Yes!
- Dynamic Creative – Very important... make sure you have this TURNED ON.
- Daily Budget – Set a daily budget. In just about every market and niche, you can successfully begin with around $10 per day. You can do more if you have a fat budget... but even then, running for a week or two at $10 a day is very effective because it is a low-risk way to gather great data.
- Audience – This is a really important part of your setup... and one of the most complicated. The key here is to make your audience as broad as possible. Give the Facebook AI system as much flexibility as you can to find your ideal audience. Because of that, I recommend that you only put limits on your audience for things that you know FOR SURE are not your audience. For example, if you sell something that is only available in Texas, you can limit the geography to Texas. Or if you have a product that is only relevant to people over 55 years old, you can limit that. Again, the trick in this section is to put as FEW limitations and parameters as possible. Let Facebook do its magic.
  - Advanced Detailed Targeting – Be sure that Advanced Detailed Targeting is TURNED ON. You'll click the "Edit" button and then check the box that describes Advanced Detailed Targeting. This gives the AI system

even more flexibility to find your ideal buyers in places that you might never have guessed they are hiding.
- Placements – Be sure "Advanced Placements" is turned on. Again, Facebook spent billions of dollars building a very clever AI system... use it to the max.
- Tracking – This section is VERY important because this is where you connect your ads to your pixel... which allows you to track everything and analyze your results.
  - Website event – Click this box and then select your Meta pixel from the drop-down menu.

Once set up, your campaign, ad set, and ads will be reviewed by Facebook's AI system. They will check for errors (like a dead URL link or wrong start date) and ad policy violations. If you have obvious ad violations, they will immediately flag it and send you a note.

If your campaign and ads are accepted, the ads will begin to run.

Your ads will go into "learning" mode... meaning, the system is sending ads to all kinds of people and in all kinds of places to figure out what the best audience and placement is.

Depending on your industry, ads, and other parameters, your ads could be in "learning" mode for a few hours to a few days. Just ignore it.

Let your ads run for at least five days without touching a thing. This will give Facebook's AI enough time to figure things out, so by then, you'll know if you have a winning ad or not.

What happens if your ad fails?

You do a little bit of advertising "tirage". You need to check these key areas and make adjustments as necessary.

- **Demand** – Is there REALLY a demand for your Transformational Idea and Offer? The best way to measure this is to look around and see if people are already buying something close to what you have to offer. Henry Ford offered the Model A in 1927. It was new and revolutionary... but the idea of faster transportation was already well-established and in high demand.

- **Copy** – Is your copy clear and persuasive, both in your ads and on your landing page? You can use the S.A.U.C.E. method to help you measure this. Have a few people score it out for you... someone who knows the industry inside and out and someone who knows very little about it, and then someone who is in the middle of obsessed and ambivalent. You'll get a good feel for how clear and persuasive it really is.
- **Dynamic Ads** – Do you have Dynamic Ads set up and do you have five versions of your copy in each section of the Facebook Ad? Running only one version of an ad in the beginning is an expensive game.
- **Pixel Settings** – Is your pixel installed correctly inside Meta and on all your landing pages? Setting this up wrong can have a dramatic effect on your tracking and teaching Meta's AI to find the right people for you.

If you have a green light on all four of these areas and are still not getting results... you need to check them again! I hope you can see me smiling. The reality is that if there is a demand... and clear copy to tell people about it... they will buy it.

Don't get caught up in the game of being the "exception" to the rule. "I did everything I was supposed to, but for some reason, my idea just didn't sell." We live in a universe of cause and effect. If your Transformational Idea is not selling, then make sure you're on track and go at it again. If there is a real demand, it will sell.

9 – Avoid Being Banned and What to Do About It If you Are

One of the best things you can do is run through Meta's eLearning course, called Ad Policies for Content Creative and Targeting. You'll need to Google that description to find it because it is buried inside the eLearning site that has like 1100 courses.

This simple course shows you examples of what is and is not acceptable to Facebook. Keep these parameters in mind when you write your copy and select your images.

As a general rule, your ads should not:

- Promise instant results—especially riches
- Have before and after comparisons—especially in the health and fitness department, they are a no-no
- Have sexually explicit images or messages
- Be racist or hateful in any way
- Be vulgar, use swear words, or imply violence
- Promote anything illegal, immoral, or unethical
- Facebook has a computer that reads all of your ads to look for obvious policy violations.

Sometimes that computer gets it wrong and rejects ads that are actually just fine. This has happened many times to me.

When that happens, you can submit it for a manual review by a real person. You do that inside your message center. Facebook will tell you when an ad has been rejected and give you a link to request a review.

But be careful... it is very likely that you'll have multiple ads rejected over time. They just seem to love rejecting ads! But if it happens too much and for serious violations, they will restrict your ad spend or ban your entire account.

If this happens, you need to get on a chat or call with Meta and walk through a resolution with them. Request an appeal and promise to comply with all policies and ask for help in understanding how to do that.

It can be frustrating to talk to a live person at Meta and they rarely give you straight answers, but it needs to be done.

Here's a pro-tip…

If your ad gets rejected a second time, after going through the review process, then delete it permanently from your account and campaign. Meta gets grumpy if you keep unapproved materials in your account. They will be happier if you comply and create a new ad.

Summary and Conclusion

There is something magical about turning on some ads in the morning and starting to see new sales come in within a few hours.

Embrace this process and get excited about it. I've given you a number of key best practices that will help you get results fast and fairly inexpensively.

Just follow the steps I've outlined and you should be fine.

If you're unsure and would like some help with the setup, reach out to us. We have top-level coaches and tech support that can help you get unstuck fast! We offer different levels of consulting, from a quick review to a complete, in-depth overhaul. You can get details by contacting us here: www.Strahes.com/ads-help.

Action Checklist

Here's a breakdown of what you need to do to get Facebook Ads running:

☐ **1 – Confirm your Identity** – Just Google "Confirm ID with Facebook". It will take you directly to the page where you can upload a valid photo ID.

- ☐ **2 – Create a Business Page** – Give Facebook as much information as you can. Add a description, address, cover photo, profile picture, etc. The more information you can add, the more "legit" FB will think you are.
    - ☐ Once you have the page fully set up, immediately make 5-10 posts.
    - ☐ After those initial posts, plan on posting another 3-7 times a week. If anyone comments on the post, take a minute to reply.
    - ☐ Your content needs to be relevant and interesting to your ideal buyer. Check out page ### for additional info on what to post.
- ☐ **3 – Set Up a Meta Business Suite** – Simply go to www.business.facebook.com, and you'll be prompted to create a Business Suite if you haven't already.
- ☐ **4 – Set Up and Install a Facebook Pixel** – Go to your Meta Business Manager. Select Business Settings > Data Sources > Pixels and follow the prompts to add a pixel. Installing a pixel on your website can be tricky depending on what platform you're using. One of the best options here is to outsource this. It just needs to be done and it is very simple for someone with a bit of tech skills.
- ☐ **5 – Set up Server Side Tracking** – You will need access to the server that hosts your website if you're going to do this yourself. If you do not have some decent tech skills, I recommend outsourcing this as well.
- ☐ **6 – Write Copy for Your Ads** – Copy is king... meaning, the words you use will have the highest impact on your conversion rates. Remember, focus on ONE benefit and keep all the supporting reasons why and feature sets focused

on that one benefit. You'll be using Dynamic Ads, so you'll need to create five versions of each element of your copy.

- ☐ Primary Text: Two short versions (30 words or less), two medium versions (100 words or less), and one long version (300+ words).
- ☐ Headline: Two short versions (40 characters or less), two medium versions (60 characters or less), and one long version (100 characters).
- ☐ Description: Two short versions, two medium versions, and one long version.

☐ **7 – Find and Edit Images for Your Ads** – Upload nine images into your Dynamic Facebook Ad, following the guidelines in this chapter.

☐ **8 – Build Your Campaign in the Facebook AdCenter** – Follow the detailed, step-by-step instructions in this chapter to build your Facebook Ads Campaign. Set your budget, then publish it! Let the campaign run for at least three days before touching it to get real feedback on performance.

☐ **9 – Avoid Being Banned** – Take a few minutes and go through Meta's eLearning course, called Ad Policies for Content Creative and Targeting.

Phase Two: Friend

Phase Two is all about inviting your ideal buyer to actually buy from you!

There is a very specific flow to this part of your funnel. You make them a series of offers, while consistently showing gratitude and appreciation for them being part of your world. You also boost their ego by telling them how smart they are for buying from you.

As you consider your approach to this phase of the game, it is good to take some time and remember that you're offering them a solution to their most pressing challenge and a way to fulfill their deepest desires. You are a blessing to them. Their life and lifestyle will be better because of you.

If you don't believe that with all your heart, you should reconsider your business.

A friend of mine runs a large-scale online business selling fasteners... nuts, bolts, screws, clasps, etc. His warehouse is massive, filled with tens of thousands of drawers filled with big bolts you might use to build a bridge or tiny screws you can use to secure the back of a watch plate.

One day, I needed a specialty bolt to fix my motorhome. That one little bolt was keeping me from driving down the road and having an amazing experience with my family.

Gratefully, he had it. That little bolt helped me fulfill a great desire I had to go on vacation with my family.

Your business has an impact on people. Own that and believe in it. Be confident and unflinching when asking for money.

There's another reason why you should be excited about asking your ideal buyers for money...

Years ago, I spoke at a conference with a man named Charlie Tremendous Jones. He is the author of more than a dozen books, including the international bestseller, Life Is Tremendous!

I was young and still held beliefs that money was evil. To be a real Saint, you had to give away all your wisdom, knowledge, and wealth (which I didn't have... I was dead-broke!) for the benefit of mankind. James Taggert-style thinking, if you've ever read Atlas Shrugged.

I was shocked to see Charlie end his amazing talk with a rather aggressive pitch to buy his books and programs. I felt like he was selling his soul and my respect for him dropped.

After he got off stage, he and I were sitting in the speaker's green room together. Being young and brash, I couldn't help myself.

"Charlie," I said. "I loved your talk, but I have to tell you, I was a little surprised and disappointed that you sold your stuff at the end. Don't you think you should just give people open access to all that stuff? I think more people would get it."

Charlie is one of the kindest, most loving people you will ever meet. When I first met him, he wrapped me up in a huge bear hug and held me for a minute.

He smiled at me and said, "I think you heard me say in my talk tonight this quote, 'You will be the same person in five years as you are today, except for the people you meet and the books you read.'

"Joshua, when you get something for free, do you value it? For example, have you ever been given a book for free that you didn't read?"

I nodded my head.

"It's the same with anything in life. When we don't sacrifice for something, when we don't pay for something, we rarely value it, consume it, or act on it.

"The worst thing in the world I could do for those people out there would be to give them all my stuff for free. They would take it home and it would collect dust. But I love them too much for that. I want them to change and grow and be happier. That is why I sell my books and courses... because I love them and want them to change.

"Do you understand?"

I nodded again and sat quietly for a long time thinking about the great lesson I'd just learned.

After a while, I went out into the foyer and bought a copy of his book. I then asked him to sign it. He did. It read, "To Joshua, You're Tremendous! Love Charlie".

I read that book and it had a great impact on my life. Mission accomplished, Charlie.

The reason we sell, sell, and sell again in Stage Two is, of course, so we can make money.

But, maybe even more importantly, it's because people value what they pay for and they tend to use what they value.

If you and I are in business, we should be in the business of bringing value to the world.

CHAPTER 5

How to Get People to Buy - Now!

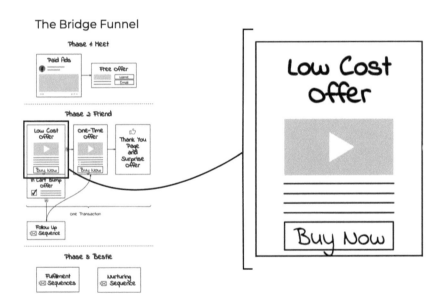

"Joshua, we need $200,000 in the next 30 days to meet all our obligations."

Carol looked tired and frustrated. She was the president of an international, pro-family organization that supports parents around the world in raising healthy, contributing children.

They do incredible work... but, like many non-profit organizations, they seemed to be constantly struggling financially.

"Carol, how many previous donors do you have on your list right now?"

"Around 120,000, if you go back about three years."

"What is the average donation when someone does give?"

"About $22."

"It seems to me," I said, "that we need to raise the average donation and get you more donors. Let's start by filling the immediate $200,000 gap with your current list, and then focus on new donor acquisition. Sounds good?"

She agreed.

The first thing we did was a survey. We discovered that many of the interests and desires of their donors were not reflected in their emails and on their website.

Additionally, they had a Free Offer—a special report that talked about three families in different parts of the world and the challenges they faced. The ideas were solid, but the copy was out of line with both the donor's language and the current focus of the company.

We updated their website and the special report.

Then we sent a letter out to their 120,000 donors, inviting people to get a free copy of the new and updated report.

Once they opted in for the report, we immediately presented them with a donation request... or a Low-Cost Offer... of just $7. We had almost 20,000 people donate within 72 hours, netting them around $140,000.

With that one effort, they were able to reach more than half of their goal.

We included other elements in that campaign, such as an In-Cart Bump Offer, a One-Time Offer, a "Thank You" Page Offer, and a Nurturing Sequence.

At the 30-day mark, they had over half a million dollars in donations, with more coming in.

The Low-Cost Offer, when done right, helps create a very powerful compounding effect. It sets them up to buy from you repeatedly over the next few minutes... and well into the future. It is their first purchase from you. Be sure to make it an enjoyable and rewarding experience!

The Low-Cost Offer is presented to them on the "Thank You" Page, immediately after they complete registration for the Free Offer.

There are nine steps to building and deploying your Low-Cost Offer.

1 – Define the Deliverables

When you created deliverables for the Free Offer, I told you to tell them what to do, not show them how to do it.

It is time to show them how. The Low-Cost Offer is all about helping them know exactly how to solve their challenge and fulfill their desires.

But, there's a catch... **If you try to give them more of what they just signed up for, your conversion rates will be very low.**

For example, with my company that trains copywriters, Copywriter Marketer, one of our top Free Offers is "10 Predictors of Success as a Writer" (you can see it here: www.10Predictors.com). The download is a report that gives a summary of the 10 things that all successful freelance copywriters should know and do.

When we first launched it, our Low-Cost Offer was a mini-training course by the same name. Essentially, we said, "Hey, you are interested in knowing about the 10 keys to being a successful freelance copywriter, so here's a video course on exactly what you just downloaded!"

And... it flopped.

The reason is obvious to me now, but it wasn't back then. I said to myself, "All the gurus told me to sell more of what is already selling well. I did that... so, why did it flop?"

Have you ever had a really annoying itch on your nose? I have. It drives me crazy... until I scratch it... then I totally forget about it (until it comes back days or weeks later).

That was exactly what was happening.

They had an itch to know what it really took to be a successful freelance copywriter. I scratched that itch and they were good for a while. They certainly didn't need to pay $7 to scratch the same itch they just had scratched for free!

The deliverable on your Low-Cost Offer (and you'll see this pattern over and over again) needs to be something valuable to them, that fulfills the core desire, but scratches a slightly different "itch".

How to Define a Deliverable That Will Sell

Now that you know why the ideas behind your Low-Cost are so vital, let's talk about how to uncover the deliverables that have the highest demand in your market.

To do that, I will use the copywriter niche as an example. The questions and process relate to every industry.

In the case of freelance copywriters, the core desire is:

"Get wealthy working for myself, doing something I love—writing."

My job in building a business is to think of all the steps and secrets along the path that help them fulfill that core desire. For Copywriter Marketer, those steps look like this, in part:

1. Understand the big picture. Do they really have the skills and desire to live the freelance copywriter life?
2. What specific skills do they need?
3. How will they acquire and master those skills?

4. What industries hire copywriters? How much do they pay?
5. How do you get someone to hire you as a new freelance writer?
6. What does the business end of a freelance writing business look like? (Contracts, legal structure, bank accounts, taxes, etc.)
7. How do you scale up to make serious money as a freelance writer?

See how there is a progression of ideas and desires? That list could be broken down into even smaller parts. For example:

- There are 10 main copywriting skills you must have to make decent money freelance writing. One of them is "writing persuasive headlines". You could break that down like this:
  - Story headlines
  - Offer headlines
  - Curiosity headlines
  - Social proof headlines
  - Direct and indirect headlines
- We could also take the top 22 industries that hire freelance copywriters. For each industry, you could outline the following information:
  - Detail who the decision makers are
  - Outline what they look for in a writer
  - List how much they pay for different projects
  - Create a glossary of what kind of jargon they use
- We can also look at it from a hands-on perspective.
  - What tools do you need to be successful?
  - What should my daily routines and schedules look like?
- How do I manage my mindset so I can have the courage, confidence, and resilience to win... because freelance writing is

a lonely, painful gig sometimes. Looking at mindset, you could identify topics such as:
- Environment
- Daily routines
- Self-talk and awareness
- Goal setting
- Physical health
- Mental Wellness

What I'm doing here is a process I call "Thin Slicing". You consider the full, big picture of the journey a person has to take to overcome their challenge and fulfill their desires.

Then, you zoom in on each step and get very granular. Take the flat, two-dimensional outline and make it a living, breathing, four or five or six-dimensional model.

Each level and each dimension can represent an "itch" that your ideal buyer needs to scratch at some point or another.

The better you understand this journey, the better you will be able to serve them and lead them along to success.

You'll also have the ability to almost infinitely increase the Lifetime Customer Value of your ideal buyer. Like with my Apple example on page ##, you'll be there at every stage of their journey, ready to help them with the next steps.

I use this information to help them along their Transformational Journey. Each step can become a place where you both strengthen your relationships with your ideal buyer and invite them to buy more stuff from you.

Here are the key questions I ask myself when building out offers for myself and my clients:

1. What is the Transformational Journey—i.e. the core desire—my ideal buyer wants to take?

2. What are the major stages in that journey?
3. Looking at each major stage, what are the steps involved?
   A. What do they need to **know**?
   B. **Who** do they need to associate with or connect with?
   C. What **tools** and resources do they need?
   D. What **skills** do they need to master?
   E. What **mindset**, motivation, and personal image do they need?
   F. What **obstacles** and challenges will they face along the way?
   G. What **victories** and joys await them?
4. What solutions do I have or can create for them to help them in their journey?
5. Here's another way to look at it... when creating any kind of offer, consider these categories.

The Unlimited Offer System

1. **Knowledge** - What knowledge, secrets, or data can you give them?
2. **Relationships** - What do you know about relationships that can transform their life?
3. **Tools** - What tools and resources do you have or can create to make their journey easier and more rewarding?
4. **Skills** - What skills do they need to progress? How can you help them master these skills faster and more effectively than anyone else?
5. **Mindset** - What is the attitude and winning mindset they need to adopt to reach their goals and fulfill their deepest desires?

6. **Obstacles** - What are the key obstacles they will face? Can you identify and demystify them so that they're no longer frightening or overwhelming?
7. **Victories** - What are the key milestones and key success indicators along their journey? What can they hope to achieve?

When you see your business through the lens of these seven categories, you realize that you have an unlimited number of deliverables and offers you can make.

The key is to offer them in the order and timing that your ideal buyer needs and wants them.

Back to our freelance copywriter example...

Instead of offering video training on the 10 Predictors of Success, I asked myself, "If they read the 10 Predictors, and still want to be a copywriter, what's the next thing they really need? And what is the next thing they THINK they really need?"

I knew those two things—what they need and what they think they need—are not always the same.

I knew from my experience that the thing they REALLY needed was a client. Nothing sharpens your skills faster... or helps you feel more confident... than a paying client.

After doing some interviews, surveys, and research, I realized that new freelance copywriter hopefuls lack confidence in their skills and don't believe that anyone will hire them. So, they think they need skills (and usually lots of them!) and a certificate (lots of those, too!) to win.

I created a mini-course Low-Cost Offer called "The Perfect Article", and it sells wonderfully well. It was the next step in their knowledge journey... the next "itch" that needed to be scratched.

Take time to consider the Transformational Journey and look at each stage of the journey through the lens of the seven categories.

The most effective offers help your ideal buyer have success at each stage of the journey, using one or more of the seven categories.

Change things up on them. Keep your offers new and innovative. As Bob Iger, former CEO of Disney, likes to say:

> "Innovate or die, and there's no innovation if you operate out of fear of the new or untested." ~ Bob Iger

If you give them a Knowledge offer, make the next offer a Skill or Tool offer or Relationship offer.

Each step of the funnel should move them toward fulfilling their core desire and be something different and unique.

2 – Choose the Format

The format options of your offers are basically the same at each stage of the funnel. As a reminder, your options are:

- **Written** – Think of a book, textbook, guide, manual, etc. Write it up, format it, add some lovely pictures and graphs, and sell it!
- **Video** – This is you, or someone else, standing in front of a camera. Think master class, virtual classroom, talking head, PowerPoints, etc.
- **Audio** – Think audiobook, podcast, interviews, radio theater, etc. Anything where they are listening.
- **Tool** – Software, hardware, worksheets, templates, forms, scripts, apps, etc. Any practical thing they can use to actually get the job done
- **Live Interaction** – Think coaching (private and group), in-person and virtual events, masterminds, networking groups, etc. Live, real-time, no-safety-net fun stuff!

Like with your deliverables, you should change up the format you offer them... while always staying focused on helping them achieve their core desire.

3 – Create the Low-Cost Offer

The creation of this Low-Cost Offer will be much the same as the process you used to create the Free Offer:

- **Write It or Record it** – The #1 secret here is to set non-negotiable appointments with yourself to get it done. Don't leave this to chance. Book the time and make it a priority. Give your best thinking and best efforts here.
- **Edit and Shine It Up** – Don't hesitate to have someone else help you with this. Outsource it, delegate it, get help. This is a valuable resource that will bring you money for many years to come. Freelance help is more abundant and cheaper today than ever before in the history of the world. Make use of it to get your manuscript edited, clean up those videos, and make your audio sound amazing. You can find a list of recommended freelancers in your bonus materials.
- **Peer Review** – Remember to have those three groups review your stuff... a mentor/expert, your ideal buyer, and someone that is totally unaware.

Refer to the chapter on creating your Free Offer for more details on this.

The question often comes up... ***How long and involved should a Low-Cost Offer be?***

I want to encourage you to end, right now and forever more, this debate in your mind.

Length is not a major factor in any of this. There is no magic number of pages or minutes.

The real magic lies in the quality of content and delivering on promises. How long does it take for you to help your ideal buyer move to the next step in their journey? That's how long it should be... and no more.

Don't cut out anything just to make it a certain length. And be willing to cut out everything that is not 100% needed to make it effective and to fulfill its purpose.

As a general rule, most non-fiction, how-to books are around 70,000 words, or about 150 pages... but Perry Marshall has a best-seller that is less than 30 pages... and Mark Ford has a 300-page best-seller.

Video courses are typically 3-7 videos, around 10-30 minutes each... but Brendon Burchard has a massive course with over 30 videos, some being over an hour long and it has made him millions.

So, don't get hung up on time. Just deliver the goods and help your ideal buyer get to the next step on their journey.

4 – Write the Sales Page Copy and Video Script

In Phase One, you created a Free Offer and a "Thank You" Page that your ideal buyer saw immediately after signing up for the Free Offer.

Now that you have a Low-Cost Offer, you will send them to the Offer Page instead of directly to the "Thank You" Page.

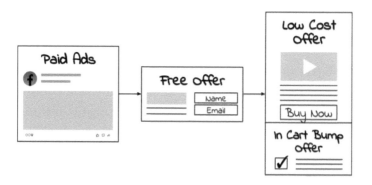

The best-performing Low-Cost Offer pages have a short video and a little sales copy. This is an impulse buy. It targets a known desire and presents a relatively well-known solution. Make it easy for them to say "Yes!"

This step is all about taking time to write! You will first write your sales page. This will allow you to hammer out the key, compelling ideas.

From there, you can use those ideas to draft your video script.

As you write the copy for the video and sales letter, be sure to go back to Chapter 3 and review the S.A.U.C.E method and the Top 8 Persuasive Desires.

The goal here is to get them to spend some money with you—anything... usually between $1 and $10.

Here are script templates and best practices you can use for the video scripts and sales copy:

In most cases, a short video (usually between two and eight minutes) of some kind performs the best for one-click offers.

Free Offer Video Script

NOTE: Before I give you the video script, just know that you don't have to use video on this page. But, it is VERY helpful and will increase your conversion rates when done right.

If you don't use a video here, you can make your sales copy a little longer, using the script outlined below.

But, if you can do it, I strongly recommend a video. It does not need to be perfect. You don't need a ton of expensive equipment... in fact, most smartphones have a camera and mic that will work just fine for raw, simple videos (which sell great!). I give you video best practices below.

Your sales video script should follow this template:

1. **Congratulate and Appreciate** – Validate that they made a great choice by getting the Free Offer from you.
2. **Special Desirable Offer** – Mention that you have a special offer for them, tailored just for them.
3. **This Page Only** – Mention the offer and price is this page only
4. **State the Problem/Pain** – Remind them of a major pain point you know they have
5. **State the Solution** – Clearly define your solution.
6. **Give Offer Details Without a Price** – State the exact offer, what they get, what benefits they enjoy. However, don't mention price—yet.
7. **Proof Points** – Cite a case study, quote a customer, reference a study, etc. Prove your solution will work.
8. **Price Stack** – Quickly demonstrate the value. "Price Stack", meaning list all the stuff they will get, the value they are getting, and name the retail price. Then drop the special sale price. You want to make the discount around 90%. Make it insanely irresistible for them... and profitable for you.

9. **Call to Action** – Tell them exactly how to order. Usually, that involves simply clicking the big, fat button under the video.
10. **Repeat Scarcity** – Repeat how limited the offer is, both in terms of price and availability.
11. **Add a Bonus** – Toss in a bonus of some kind to make the offer even more insanely irresistible to them.
12. **Repeat Call to Action** – One final call to action (CTA). Be specific. Two kinds of CTAs usually work very well here. The Crossroads CTA where you tell them they are at a crossroads where they can do nothing and get nothing, or take action and enjoy the benefits. Or the simple Assumptive Command CTA, where you look them in the eyes and say something like, "This is the best thing for you right now. Order now and I'll see you on the other side."

You can find a few script examples in the bonus materials.
Here's a template for the sales copy:

- **Eyebrow Copy** – This is the copy at the top of the page. This should confirm their order of the Free Offer, assure them it is on the way, and congratulate them. "Thank you! [FREE REPORT NAME] Is on Its Way! Just One More Step... Watch the Short Video Below..."
- **Headline** – State ONE big promise/benefit they will get. Be direct and clear. This should be a benefit you know they want and hint at a clear solution.
- **Video** – Insert the video directly below the headline, if you're using a video.
- **Proof Elements** – You can use a counter with the number of buyers/members in your world, icons of companies you've serviced, years in business, credentials, etc.—anything that helps to build trust and give you more credibility.

- **Sub-Headline** – Restate your offer and the one benefit they get.
- **Promise Copy** – In a short paragraph, outline the one core benefit and add a few supporting elements. This paragraph should lead into and introduce the bullet points.
- **Bullet Points** – World Class copywriter, Gary Bencivenga, called bullet points "fascinations"... meaning, they were written in a way that totally fascinated the reader and made them hungry to buy. You should have 3-5 bullet points. They should identify a feature and clearly define the benefit. "The number one secret to being paid twice as much as other writers is found on page 89 of your PDF guide."
- **Social Proof** – Include 3-5 testimonials or short case studies that validate your claims and strengthen your promises and benefits.
- **Price Stack** – Outline the value they get with this offer and name the retail price. Then state the discounted price. Again, this should be around a 90% discount. Make the retail price $97 and the Offer Price at just $7. These are proven price points.
- **Call to Action** – Tell them exactly what to do next. "Click on the button below to get instant access."
- **Bonus** – Include a value-add bonus. One very powerful technique is to make sure that the retail value of the bonus is worth as much or more than the Flagship Offer itself. If the retail value of the Low-Cost Offer is $97... then add a bonus that would normally cost them $97 or more. The bonus should be a different offer category than the Low-Cost Offer. For example, if the Low-Cost Offer is a video course, this could be a workbook to go along with it. It could be an audio of the program or a transcript. Make it something simple but valuable.

- **Guarantee** – Take all the risk away from them. If they don't like the offer, for any reason, you'll instantly refund their money and let them keep the purchase... or something like that.
- **Call to Action** – Restate the call to action. Be as clear as possible
- **Social Proof** – Add 2-3 more social proof elements such as social media comments, testimonials, or case studies.

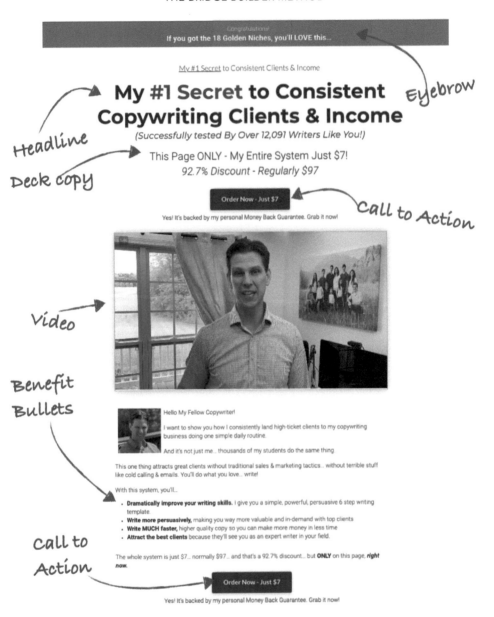

In addition to the persuasive copywriting insights I gave you in Chapter 3, here are a few more insights on the copy that will help you. These are specific to the One-Time Offer because as you go through the funnel process, different relationship levels require slightly different communication elements.

Short, Compelling Copy

This is an impulse buy that you will strategically craft to meet an exact, known need for your buyer. It should logically make sense to them, within the framework of the desires that drove them to the first purchase. Their awareness of the problem or the solution (or both) should be extremely high.

This is NOT the time to introduce a new concept, product, or service to them that requires education on the benefits of the products and its benefits.

Because of these factors, the copy should be very short. In most cases, make less than 500 total words on the page. This includes testimonials, proof elements, headlines, call to action, etc.

If you use a video, you can still get away with around 500 words on this page, but it can also be much shorter—around 200 words often is enough. (This paragraph is 35 words.)

Huge Order Now Button

If you use a video, you should have a very large order button directly under the video.

If you do not use a video, the large order button should be to the right of the copy. If you can do it, the order button should follow them as they scroll down. Around the order button, restate the benefits and the scarcity/urgency elements.

Escape Button

Be sure to give them a clear escape button... meaning, show them clearly how they decline the offer and move on with their purchase.

Sometimes people make this tiny little text under the order button that needs a high-powered microscope to read. This is actually a huge mistake.

First, it makes people feel trapped and manipulated.

Second, it often results in someone ordering by accident or out of frustration. This will increase your refund and chargeback rates. That will cost you money and might eventually get your merchant account shut down.

Third, and most important, an escape button gives the buyer a feeling of power. We all like choice. No one likes to be forced into something.

So, be sure to show them that you are so confident that this is a great, irresistible offer, that you can dangle the "No Thanks" button or text in front of them, but they'll buy anyway. Give them the power to say "No" and you'll find that they actually say "Yes" much more often.

5 – Shoot and Edit the Video (Optional... but SOOO Powerful!)

If you are comfortable with video, this will be easy for you.

If you have not done video before, don't be intimidated by this step. A raw, simple video done sincerely and with genuine intent to help the ideal buyer on their journey will be perfect.

The important part is that they hear from YOU. You, being your sincere, genuine... and yes, maybe even scared, nervous, and unprofessional self... is much better than hiring a fake actor or having someone less passionate stand in for you.

You are doing this because you want to help transform their lives. You're passionate about this and believe it will change the world. Just turn the phone on and let all that conviction flow from you.

Years ago, I did a group consulting session with some clients over video. There were about 30 people on the call. One of them, Sam, had a powerful message and wanted to jump into the personal development space. He was a very shy, private, and reserved person.

"Joshua, I just don't know what to say on camera. I'm thinking about having someone else do the pitch."

"Sam, can you tell me why you got into the personal development space? Why do you want to get your insights out there?"

For the next 10 minutes, Sam literally exploded with energy. He told me all about his childhood, his first marriage, his drug addictions, and all the crazy stuff he'd gone through.

Then, with a few questions from me, he detailed his transformation and journey of healing and power. It was so intense and so emotional... and I recorded the whole thing!

"Sam, did you see what you just did? You stopped thinking about being on camera and just shared with me your story and your passion. That is the perfect way to do this video."

"I know, but I could never do it on video. I get all locked up knowing I'm being recorded."

"Sam, I hate to tell you this, but you just did it all on video. I recorded the whole thing! You can use this recording or have someone at the office ask you those same questions with a camera recording. You can do this!"

He did and it was a great success!

I've included some best practices for video production in your bonus materials. Refer to those before going at it.

The video should be around 3-10 minutes. Follow the script outline I gave you in section 4 and you'll do great!

Editing Your Video

Now that you've shot your Low-Cost Offer video, it needs to be edited.

The best option is to find someone that knows what they are doing and outsource it. It is a great investment. If you want to edit the video yourself, follow these simple guidelines:

- Trim the front and the back. Videos don't start instantly and don't end instantly. You have a second or two of you staring blankly at the camera or saying, "Is it on? Are we recording?" You'll want to cut those parts out.
- Adjust lighting and sound if needed.
- Put a call to action link or statement in the video as a title overlay. "Order Now" should pop up at the bottom of the video when you tell them the price. You can also include a URL if it is easy to remember. "www.18Niches.com/win" or something like that. Long, ugly domains shouldn't be displayed because no one can remember them.

6 – Set Up Your Payment System

You need a way to take people's money when they decide they want to do business with you.

To keep things simple, your two best options are:

- **PayPal** – You can get a free account. Just about every CRM in the world integrates with PayPal. Kartra and ClickFunnels allow you to set up PayPal with just a few clicks.
- **Stripe** – Stripe has revolutionized merchant accounts. You can be up and running, collecting credit cards online within a few hours.

I recommend you have both of these, but you can get started with just PayPal.

Stripe is very easy to set up if you have already formed an LLC and a business bank account. If you're still working on those things, just use PayPal for now.

You will need to set these up inside your CRM so that they integrate with your shopping cart.

7 – Set Up the Product in Your CRM

Each CRM has a slightly different product setup. In general, you'll need the following:

- **Product Description** – Make this short and benefit-rich.
- **Price** – You can enter a retail price and special Offer Price. Most CRMs allow you to set multiple price points for the same product.
- **Image** – Boxshot, logos, icons, or pictures representing the offer.
- **Library or Membership** – You will need to set up their library or membership area. This is the "members only" area of your website that requires a username and password to access. Inside, they will find all the programs, tools, resources, etc. that they've purchased from you. They will have a single sign on so that one username and password will get them access to everything.

8 – Build the Offer Page

Your CRM should have a template for an Offer Page. The layout is very similar to the Free Offer page, with the following structure:

- Eyebrow Copy
- Headline
- Video
- Order Button
- Proof Elements
- Sub-headline
- Body Copy and Bullet Points
- Call to Action with Order Button
- Testimonials
- Guarantee
- Call to Action with Order Button
- Social Proof
- Order Button

For more details on the elements of this Offer Page, refer to the section on writing the Sales Copy and Video Script in this chapter. You can also take a look at the section on creating the Opt-In Form and Page in Chapter 3.

9 – Create the Order Page

When someone clicks on the "Order Now" button, they will be taken to an order page. You will need the following elements on this page.

Oftentimes, an order page is a ⅔ split page, with the contact information form and payment form on the left 2/3rds and the Low-Cost Offer headline description, summary, and social proof elements in the right-hand 1/3rd area.

- **Headline** – Typically placed on the right-hand side, above an image or logo of the Low-Cost Offer. This is usually the name of the Low-Cost Offer. You can add a tagline or benefit statement.
- **Image/Icon/Logo** – Something to represent your offer.
- **Confirmation Copy** – Restate the benefits and what a great choice they've made. Sometimes this copy is written in first-person, such as, "Yes! Please send me... "
- **Bullet Point Summary** – Include 3-5 bullet points outlining the features and what they are getting.
- **Social Media** – If you have room, it is great to include a quote or testimonial right next to the contact information form.
- **Contact Information Form** – Form that asks for name, email, phone, etc. This will be automatically generated by your CRM.
- **In-Cart Bump Offer** – You have not built this out yet, but when you do, this is where it goes. Some CRMs put it after the payment information and some put it in the right-hand column. More details on the In-Cart Bump Offer in the next chapter.
- **Payment Information** – Enter their form of payment.
- **Acceptance of Terms** – Be sure to include this. You should have a terms and conditions page that includes confirmation that they actually want to purchase the Low-Cost Offer. This little bit of copy and the button they have to click can save you a ton of legal headaches and prevent losing chargeback decisions. Your CRM can add it automatically, you just need to supply the copy. The easy way to do this is to find a website you've bought things from and swipe their Terms... update them to fit your needs... done. Very simple.

THE BRIDGE BUILDER METHOD

- **Submit Order Button** – Big, clear-to-see "Order Now" button. On this page, don't get creative with the language on the order button. You can play with that on the Free Offer Button, but here it just needs to be "Order Now" or "Submit Order".

10 – Create a "Thank You" Page

Once they complete the purchase, you will send them directly to a "Thank You" Page"... at least until you get your One-Time Offer system set up. Once the OTO process is set up, you'll send them to the next offer.

You might be tempted to wait until you have the One-Time Offer done to build and release your Low-Cost Offer. There is a TON of wisdom in building each piece of your funnel and immediately deploying it. You gather important data, you start building your ads, and you generate some income while you're working on your other elements.

So, don't wait. Build a "Thank You" Page and start selling your Low-Cost Offer immediately.

The best part is that you can make this very simple. Duplicate the "Thank You" Page you created in Chapter 3 with the Free Offer and updated a little based on your Low-Cost Offer.

The "Thank You" Page for the Low-Cost Offer has all the same elements as the Free Offer "Thank You" Page. As a reminder, here are the elements we talked about in Chapter 3...

- **Headline** – This is a congratulations note affirming that they have made a great decision. Be sure to mention the name of the Free Offer so that they know they are in the right place.
- **Image or Graphic** – Include an image of yourself (or the expert/guru if that's not you) and/or a box shot of the Free Offer they just registered for. A picture of yourself is easiest. If you want to include an image of the Free Offer, just copy the cover and put it here... but keep it simple!
- **Access Information** – Tell them how they access their Free Offer. Typically, you'll send them an email with an access link and password information. Something simple like... "An email

is on its way to you right now with full access info" is good enough.
- **Call to Action** – In the future, you'll invite them to go deeper into your funnel (more on that later), but for now, just invite them to engage in your world. This could be an invitation for them to follow you on social media, read an article, listen to your podcast, or send you an email with feedback/a testimonial. Simply put it at the end under a sub-head that reads, "Here's the Next Step…"

11 – Write and Set Up Access and Consumption Emails

After they buy the Low-Cost Offer, they need to immediately get two emails from you. The Welcome and Access Email and the Consumption Email(s).

Welcome and Access Email

This is NOT the same "Welcome to the Family" email. They already received that one from you… in fact, they might have received it just minutes before buying the Low-Cost Offer. So, you don't need to repeat that.

But, they do need a brief "Welcome to the [NAME OF THE LOW-COST OFER]". Here is a simple template for this email:

- **Subject Line:** [NAME], here's your access to [LOW-COST OFFER].
- Salutation with their name: "Hi [NAME]!
- **Welcome and Congratulations:** "Thank you for ordering [LOW-COST OFFER]. You made a great decision. Inside, you'll find… [BULLET POINTS WITH BENEFITS]."

- **Benefits Bullet Points:** Restate the benefits in 3-5 very brief bullet points.
- **Access Information:** If you use Kartra or ClickFunnels, the username and password to access their purchase will be the exact same username and password they need to access their Free Offer. The CRM will provide you with a little bit of code called a merge field to give them that information here again. Usually, it looks something like this: {first_name} or {login_access}.
- **Call to Action:** Invite them to do something. Read a specific area in the program, check out another product, follow you on social media channels, register for a webinar, etc. Always, always, always, invite them to take action of some kind.
- **Close:** End with your unique greeting and name. I usually use something like, "To Your Best Life, Joshua".

Consumption Email

People like for you to do the work for them. They love being helped each step along the way. You can both boost their ego and help them have greater success on their journey by sending them 1-3 emails that help them consume the Low-Cost Offer.

Here's a simple template you can use:

- **Subject Line:** Did you see [feature or benefit]?
- Salutation: "Hi [NAME]!"
- **1-3 Pro-Tips:** I call them "pro-tips", but you can call them anything you'd like. Think of it like this... if you were brand-new to your world, what do you wish someone would point out or help with? Share those things with them. These suggestions can include:
    - Highlights of the best or highest-leverage areas of your Low-Cost Offer

- Insights from other users on making the most of your offer
- Extra tidbits that you didn't include in the core program
- Suggestions on how to go through the Low-Cost Offer
- **Call to Action:** Invite them to take one specific action.
- **Close:** Closing salutation.

Again, you should write up 1-3 of these and put them on auto-send in your CRM. The purchase of your Low-Cost Offer will trigger them. These little emails do wonders for customer loyalty, increase retention rate, reduce refunds, and increase future sales.

They show you care and are sincerely interested in helping your ideal buyer overcome their challenges and fulfill their desires.

12 – Write a Follow-Up Email Sequence for Non-Buyers

I have shocking news for you... not everyone that sees your offer will buy. If you do a good job with everything I've outlined, you could be proud of a 10% conversion rate... even 5% would be totally acceptable.

But, how would you like to boost that to upwards of 20%-40%? The way to move the needle like that is to send out a Follow-Up Email Sequence to all the non-buyers. Sometimes this is called a "Cart Abandonment Sequence" because it goes to people who look but don't buy. Since I like the idea of following up with them to continue building the relationship, I'll keep calling it a "Follow-Up Sequence".

Remember, you have their email address because they signed up for the Free Offer AND you have their permission to contact them.

So, make the most of it.

You know they have seen your Low-Cost Offer and you also know they didn't buy. This means you can now have a VERY specific conversation with them.

Let me show you how powerful this can be...

Client Case Study

One of our clients, a new personal development company, had a Free Offer that included an online lifestyle and personal development assessment.

After their ideal customers received the assessment results, they had the opportunity to purchase a Low-Cost Offer for just under $10. It was a training module that retailed for around $100.

The conversion rates for this offer were averaging around 7%. Not bad, but not great.

We implemented a simple, three-part follow-up sequence.

One of the challenges was that people wanted to take some time to go through the assessment, which was packed full of really great insights and suggestions. Buying a training course immediately after that was like drinking from a firehose.

The follow-up sequence gave them time to digest the assessment results, but didn't give them so much time that they lost enthusiasm for the program.

Within a week of implementing the follow-up sequence, conversion rates for the Low-Cost Offer shot to 29%, or about 1 in 3! At $10, by itself, this was not a major game-changer... but when you factored in the increased revenues created by the In-Cart Bump Offer and the conversion rates for the One-Time Offers, it transformed their business.

They went from around 400 paying students to over 75,000 as of this writing... and growing.

They have since been bought up by one of the world's largest personal development companies and generate more than $100 million in sales each year.

The follow-up email sequence was the kingpin that allowed them to realize this growth. It has a major domino effect because it puts more buyers into your funnel. It also gives you a faster return on ad spend, which allows you to spend more and acquire customers faster.

Here's the pattern for the follow-up email sequence:

Email #1 – Offer Extended

Let them know that you've decided to extend the special price and offer it to them. They have 48 hours to buy before it goes back to the regular retail price.

Send one hour after they finish the funnel sequence.

Note that if they don't buy the Low-Cost Offer, you will NOT send them through the other One-Time Offers. Instead, you just send them to the standard Thank You Page. This costs you a little money in immediate sales because some people would purchase your One-Time Offer and not purchase your Low-Cost Offer. But, doing it this way makes you more long-term money. It shows respect for your ideal buyer and increases their trust in you.

Here's a simple template for follow-up email #1:

- **Subject Line:** Offer Extended for 48 Hours Only.
- Salutation: "Hi [NAME].
- **Offer and Urgency:** "I noticed that you did not grab [LOW-COST OFFER NAME]. This is one of our most popular programs. Because you might not have seen it or realized what it was, I'm extending the 90% discount... but only for 48 hours... then it goes back to full price.
- **Call to Action:** Include a button or link here that sends them to the Low-Cost Offer sales page, the same one they saw after they signed up for the Free Offer.

- **Benefit Details:** Outline the benefits in a few short bullet points. You can use the same copy from the Low-Cost sales page.
- **Call to Action:** Text or button sending them to the sales page.
- **Value Stack:** List the value of everything they are getting. List the retail price. Contrast it with the sales offer.
- **Social Proof:** Include 1-3 testimonials or quotes. Can be pulled from the sales page.
- **Guarantee:** Restate the guarantee. Can be pulled from the sales page.
- **Call to Action:** Another text or button sending them to the sales page.
- Closing Salutation
- **PS with Bonus:** Include a postscript that restates the bonus you offered them on the sales page.
- **Call to Action:** Include one final button or text inviting them to take action.

Email #2 – Social Proof

In the second email, you will give them massive social proof. Really help them feel like they are missing out on something special.

Send email #2 on the morning of day two, around 7 am or 8 am.

Here is a template you can use for email #2.

- **Subject Line:** Offer Extended for 48 Hours Only.
- **Eyebrow Urgency:** At the top of the email, before the salutation, include a brief bit of urgency copy. If you can, include a countdown timer. The timer should end that night at 11:59 pm. "90% Discount Ends Tonight. Order Now!"
- Salutation: "Hi [NAME].
- **Social Proof Intro:** "I know you're considering my 90% discount offer for [LOW-COST OFFER NAME]. I thought

you might like to hear from a few of our other customers…" Then include 3-5 short testimonials. Include a call to action in between each testimonial.
- **Call to Action:** Include a button or link here that sends them to the Low-Cost Offer sales page, the same one they saw after they signed up for the Free Offer.
- **Benefit Details:** Restate the benefits in a few short bullet points. You can use the same copy from the Low-Cost sales page.
- **Call to Action:** Text or button sending them to the sales page
- **Value Stack:** List the value of everything they are getting. List the retail price. Contrast it with the sales offer.
- **Guarantee:** Restate the guarantee. Can be pulled from the sales page
- **Call to Action:** Another text or button sending them to the sales page.
- Closing Salutation
- **PS with Bonus:** Include a postscript that restates the bonus you offered them on the sales page.
- **Call to Action:** Include one final button or text inviting them to take action.

Email #3 – Last Call

This email is very short and simple. It informs them that the 90% discount ends that day at 11:59 pm.

You will send this email on the evening of day two at around 7 pm or 8 pm.

Here is a simple template you can use for email #3:

- **Subject Line:** Ends in a few hours… you coming?
- **Eyebrow Urgency:** At the top of the email, before the salutation, include a brief bit of urgency copy. If you can,

include a countdown timer. The timer should end that night at 11:59 pm. "90% Discount Ends Soon. Order Now!"
- Salutation: Hi [NAME]!
- **Final Offer Intro:** "Your 90% discount ends in just a few hours. I really don't want you to miss this, so I'm sending you one final invite to join us…"
- **Call to Action:** Include a button or link here that sends them to the Low-Cost Offer sales page—the same one they saw after they signed up for the Free Offer.
- **Benefit Details:** Restate the benefits in a few short bullet points. You can use the same copy from the Low-Cost sales page.
- **Call to Action:** Text or button sending them to the sales page.
- **Value Stack:** List the value of everything they are getting. List the retail price. Contrast it with the sales offer.
- **Guarantee:** Restate the guarantee. Can be pulled from the sales page.
- **Call to Action:** Another text or button sending them to the sales page.
- Closing Salutation
- **PS with Bonus:** Include a postscript that restates the bonus you offered them on the sales page.
- **Final Call to Action:** Include one final button or text inviting them to take action.

You'll notice that these email templates are very similar. You change up the first part of the email and you can leave the rest as-is, with a few minor tweaks.

Conclusion

"I think we should run a new campaign to every registered voter in Montana and ask them to donate $1 to your US senate race."

Mike looked at me like I was crazy.

"But it will cost us at least $1 to print and mail the letter. That sounds like a total waste of time."

"Didn't you have loss leaders in the beauty salon business?"

He nodded his head.

"Our problem right now is that we don't have enough donors. The ones we have are doing great, but we need 10 times our cash on hand and we can only squeeze current donors so much. The only way forward is with new blood.

"If we can get them to donate something as small as $1, we can follow up with bigger requests and move them over to our online system. At the least we'll break even," I said.

Nodding his head, he agreed. "But keep the costs as low as possible. And I want you writing that letter, not some copywriter in a political consulting sweatshop, you hear me?"

I wrote the letter. We printed it on slightly cheaper paper and got a huge bulk discount on postage. Our cost was just under $0.85 per mailing and we mailed just over 50,000 letters.

It was a very Low-Cost Offer and a $50,000 risk that the campaign really couldn't afford.

We had a 27% response rate, or about 13,500 new donors. We asked for emails in the donation forms, both physical and online. We also asked for a little more, if they felt so generous... and many did. In total, we averaged an initial $3.50 per donor... or around $47,250.

I was delighted to report to Mike that we'd only lost an initial $2,750 on the campaign.

Here was where the real magic kicked in...

With our other fundraising efforts, I knew our average donor lifetime value was just over $41. In other words, I'd just taken an initial loss of $2,750 to make around $553,500. You can't get that kind of return on Wall Street (at least not legally).

That is just one illustration of the power of a Low-Cost Offer. A well-done Low-Cost Offer allows you to minimize your out-of-pocket expenses and acquire new buyers... not new free registrants... buyers.

Action Checklist

- ☐ **1 – Define the Deliverables** – The Low-Cost Offer should be distinctly different from the Free Offer. Make sure that it aligns with their core desires and is insanely valuable and user-friendly. This first purchase is extremely important for a long-term relationship.

- ☐ **2 – Choose the Format** – Some formats to choose from are: Written, Video, Audio, Tools, Live Interaction. Any of these different modalities can make a wonderful Low-Cost Offer. Best practice to present this in a different modality than the Free Offer.

- ☐ **3 – Create the Low-Cost Offer** – Simply set a time and create. Whether you're writing, recording video, or creating an online tool, you need to set a non-negotiable time to get it done. Make sure to have it peer reviewed when you finish. As a reminder, don't get hung up on time. Just take however long you need to deliver the goods and help your ideal buyer get to the next step on their journey.

- ☐ **4 – Write the Sales Page Copy and Video Script** – Remember... use short, compelling copy, have a huge order now button, and an escape button that's clearly visible. This will help increase your conversions.

- ☐ **5 – Shoot and Edit the Video** – This is optional, but I highly recommend it. If you have not done video before,

- ☐ **6 – Set Up Your Payment System** – I recommend setting up PayPal and Stripe for your payments, then integrating those with the CRM. If you haven't set up a business bank account, you can start with just PayPal.

- ☐ **7 – Set Up the Product in Your CRM** – Of course, the actual process will be different between platforms, but the goal here is to get your product available for sale. Be sure to test that everything works before you go live.

- ☐ **8 – Build the Offer Page** – For more details on the elements of this Offer Page, take a look at the section on creating the Opt-In Form and Page in Chapter 3. You can also refer to the section on writing the Sales Copy and Video Script in this chapter.

- ☐ **9 – Create the Order Page** – When someone decides to buy from you, they'll click on the order button on the Offer Page. Then they'll be taken to this page where they can add their payment info. Follow the guidelines in this chapter for what elements to include.

- ☐ **10 – Create the "Thank You" Page** – Once they complete the purchase, you will send them directly to a "Thank You" Page." This can be a duplicate of the "Thank You" Page" that you built for your Free Offer, with a few tweaks to make it relevant to the Low-Cost Offer.

- ☐ **11 – Write and Set Up Access and Consumption Emails** – As soon as someone buys, they need a brief "Welcome to the [NAME OF THE LOW-COST OFER]". You can also boost their ego and help them have greater success on their

(continued from previous page: don't be intimidated. A raw, simple video done sincerely and with genuine intent to help will be perfect.)

journey by sending them 1-3 emails that help them consume the Low-Cost Offer.

☐ **12 – Write a Follow-Up Email Sequence for Non-Buyers** – This is often called a "Cart Abandonment" sequence. Some people will make an instant decision to buy something from you. But more people will make that decision if you give them additional time and reasons to buy, and consistently follow up with them over a few days.

CHAPTER 6

The Secret to Triple Revenues

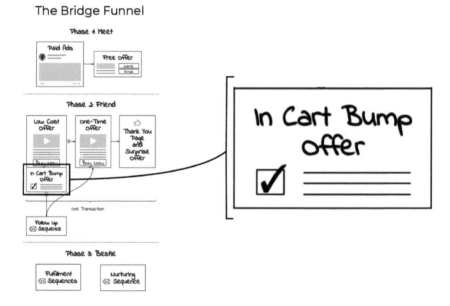

"Let me show you the one thing I did early on that allowed me to triple my ad spend and get customers faster than just about anyone in the industry."

I was sitting in a large conference room in a private and confidential mastermind. In fact, we all agreed that we would not disclose who was in the room. I'll call the speaker Alfred.

THE SECRET TO TRIPLE REVENUES

The man at the front of the room, Alfred, owns or has ownership in more than a dozen companies, most of which do over $50 million in sales and at least two that are valued at over a billion. I was all ears to hear what he was about to say!

(On a side note... the most successful and wealthiest people I have learned from have holding companies—meaning companies that own other companies. Maybe one day I'll write a book about the little-known practices of the super-rich...)

Alfred picked up a fat king-sized marker and began making a diagram on the flip chart. He was outlining one of his sales funnels. Finally, he took out a red marker and circled one element and labeled it "Bump Offer".

"How many of you are using a Bump Offer to boost your sales?"

No one raised their hands. I think today the term is a little more used, but back then, it was not common. In fact, most online carts and CRM systems didn't even offer it as a feature. Alfred had figured out a way to hack his check-out cart and code it into the payment process.

Alfred nodded his head.

"Ok, I want you to promise me that from now on, you'll include a Bump Offer every time you sell something. Make it standard practice, especially on your initial funnel. This one little box is a secret to my being able to enter different markets and quickly create profitable growth."

I was super excited to put his promise to the test.

At the time, it was costing me around $47 to acquire a customer for one of my companies.

My return on ad spend timeframe was 60 days... meaning I didn't get all of that $47 back for 60 days. That is really not bad, but I wanted to get my money back faster so I could spend it on ads. This would allow me to acquire customers much faster. The In-Cart Bump Offer was apparently the magic bullet.

We tested a number of Bump Offers ranging from $97 to $19. We found that our highest response rate was $19.

While that does not seem like a lot, it has a major ripple effect.

When a buyer makes a second small purchase commitment like this (the first being the Low-Cost Offer they just bought), they are far more likely to make another one... IF it scratches a slightly different itch, as we talked about before.

We found that the addition of the In-Cart Bump Offer increased the response rates for our One-Time Upsell and Downsell offers from around 5% to over 20%... a 300% increase.

And, as a final benefit, the Bump Offer increased our "Thank You" Page conversion rates from 1% to around 3%... another 200% increase!

Alfred was right—this was a game-changer for us. We went from having an initial customer value of around $7 to $72. This allowed us to recoup our advertising costs in under three days instead of in 60 days. Now, we could spend advertising dollars on Monday and reuse those dollars on Wednesday!

The In-Cart Bump Offer

When your ideal buyer goes to check out and enter their payment information, you will give them a simple offer. To accept the offer, all they need to do is check the box and it will be added to their total before they finalize their purchase.

THE SECRET TO TRIPLE REVENUES

Setting the Price of the Bump Offer

I have seen many price points work for the Bump Offer, but for now, you will set your Bump Offer Price at $19. After testing thousands of offers in dozens of different industries, this consistently performs the best.

Set Up Your In-Cart Bump Offer

There are seven simple steps to setting up your In-Cart Bump Offer:

1 – Define the Deliverables of Your Bump Offer

You'll get tired of hearing me say this... but it is always the first step.

What value will you give?

Why should your ideal buyer care?

Why should they spend their money on this instead of a dinner and a movie (or whatever else they would drop $20 on)?

As you consider the deliverables on the Bump Offer, remember that you need to scratch a new itch. A few key things to keep in mind...

- **VERY Short Copy** – You get about 100 words—or less—to state your offer and make it persuasive. This needs to be an offer with an instantly recognizable benefit that the buyer really wants.
- **Massive Value** – Same as with other offers, but it cannot be overstated enough. Establish huge value, sell for a small price.
- **Draw Attention** – A Bump Offer sits inside the shopping cart, usually between the contact information form and the payment information form. They click a little box to activate it. Use bright colors, arrows, and boxes to draw attention to the offer.
- **End in Mind** – As with the Free and Low-Cost Offer, you are building a relationship and leading them to larger purchases. It is an ascension model and it needs to make logical sense to them. Remember, they entered your world for a specific emotional reason. Stay within that framework.

2 – Create Your Bump Offer

Bump offers should be a different product modality than the Low-Cost Offer, scratching a slightly different itch, but still within the framework of the buyer's core desire.

This is a HUGE point that will make or break your In-Cart Bump Offer conversion rates and profits, so let me state it again…

The In-Cart Bump Offer needs to be a different category type than your Low-Cost Offer.

What I mean is this…

If your Low-Cost Offer is a book on Mediterranean Diet Secrets, your Bump Offer could be something like one of these:

- **Audiobook** – An audio version of the book. It is a different medium and it scratches the itch to consume the book on the road or while working out. The promise to fulfill the desire to be healthier, skinnier, and cooler by doing a Mediterranean diet is still the same.
- **Planning Guide** – A diet planning guide, complete with done-for-you menus. This is a practical tool. It helps the user implement the ideas from the book. The promised outcome is still the same.
- **Coaching Session** – A 30-minute consultation with a certified nutritionist to give you best practices and customize the diet. This is different from just reading a book. It is a live interaction and personalized help. The promised outcome is the same.
- **Event Tickets** – Tickets to a small group, live event, or online seminar.
- **Swag** – Hats, exercise clothes, coffee mugs, and other things to inspire them and help them have bragging rights in front of their friends. Increases motivation and helps stay committed.

Promised outcome is basically the same, with a cool social factor included.
- **Cooking Gadgets** – Cookware, serving utensils, and storage containers to make the transition to the new diet easier, more effective, and more fun. Same promised outcome.
- **Unique Food and Nutritional Supplements** – Addition of organic olive oil, vitamin or mineral supplements that make losing weight or feeling better during the dieting process. Same promised outcome, but boosted with results coming faster and easier.

All of these offers are in a different offer category than a book... but are totally congruent with the core desire for buying the book.

Shocking, No-Brainer Value

In most cases, the Bump Offer should be offered at a minimum of a 50% discount... usually 90%.

The value and desirability of the Bump Offer should be so high that clicking the little box and adding it to the order is a total no-brainer.

Apple actually does this with their AppleCare protection plan and software offers. You can get unlimited coverage on your Apple iPhone for between $7.99 and $13.99 a month. It is inexpensive and offers huge value.

Make It Profitable for You

Of course, the key here is to make sure that your Bump Offer is both insane value to the buyer... and makes you a profit.

There are no extra points in creating a Bump Offer that costs you money. The purpose of the Bump Offer is to make you money.

3 – Write the Bump Offer Copy

As I stated, you have less than 100 words to make the pitch and close the deal. Here is a simple template you can use to make it work:

- Headline – A short, very simple, clear, benefit-rich headline with ONE very big idea. NOTE: With a Bump Offer, all the copy is compressed into a single, short paragraph. That means that your "headline" is just your first sentence.
- Price Stack – Detail the retail price and then the Offer Price. Usually, you will give them a 50%-90% discount.
- Description – Tell them, briefly, what they will get. Keep it focused on the value and benefits.
- Guarantee – Take away the risk!
- Call to Action – "Check the box now to add to your order."

Here's an example of a Bump Offer we successfully use with copywriters:

> "Get ALL the tools, forms, contracts, and scripts you need to profitably run your copywriting business. Normally $149… Today only, just $19. The Professional Copywriter's Toolbox took over 10 years to develop. You get over 200 resources! Deal contracts. Email and phone scripts. Upsell process and dialogues. NDA forms. Proposal templates. And much more! Get EVERYTHING you need to run your copywriting business… for just $19. Satisfaction guaranteed—or your money back. Check the box now to add to your order!"

This is 81 words long and has sold thousands of times.

Notice that it is a set of tools… not information. It solves an immediate, known challenge, namely, "What should a job proposal look like, and if someone does want to hire me, what does the contract look like?"

This is a major concern for freelance copywriters... and one that this Bump Offer instantly solves... plus a lot more things they will need but have not thought of just yet. I'm staying one step ahead of them and giving them value. I'm building a bridge across a chasm they haven't reached yet, but will.

Here's a pro-tip for you... keep the FK score VERY low on your Bump Offer copy. As you remember, we discussed FK score in the section on creating an information product. You can calculate your FK score with tools like www.readable.io, Grammarly, or others. The lower the score, the better, but at least keep it under FK 7. The example above is FK 5.6.

4 – Set Up In the CRM

You will need to set this up as a product inside your CRM and set an automation to add it to their membership/library area once they purchase it. This is the same process you used with the Low-Cost Offer. (See page ##)

It should take you no more than 30 minutes to set that up.

5 – Add the Bump Offer to the Cart

Access the cart setup options inside your CRM. You'll find an option to add a Bump Offer (or In-Cart Offer... or some other similar language.)

Add your copy and select any design features, such as arrows, bullets, bold text, colored boxes, etc. Keep the design in harmony with your other image branding and relatable to your ideal buyer, but attention-grabbing.

A word of caution here... be sure to place the Bump Offer box after the contact information section.

A key concept behind persuasion is what renowned persuasion psychologist, Robert Cialdini, calls, "Commitment and Consistency".

As humans, we tend to stay consistent with commitments we've made. Once we start down a path, we like to stay on it.

This principle is the driving force behind what is sometimes called "Micro Commitments". The basic idea is that you help your buyer make a bunch of tiny commitments to you.

You want them to become accustomed to trusting you enough to follow your lead and accept your suggestions. When this happens, it is much more likely that they will follow through with purchases and actions you invite them to take.

This is important, not only to increase sales, but also to increase application, use, and consumption of your products and services.

Remember my conversation with Charlie "Tremendous" Jones? We are in business to bring value, solve problems, and fulfill desires. That only happens when they use our stuff. And that is more likely to happen when they look to you for leadership in their life.

Each action your buyer takes at your request increases the likelihood that they will take another.

When they fill out the contact information, that is a micro-commitment. Entering their payment information is a micro-commitment.

By placing your Bump Offer box toward the end of the process, you increase your conversion rates because you've increased the number of micro-commitments they've made to you.

6 – Access and Consumption Email

You will need to do this with every product you ever sell. Send them a brief email telling them how to access their purchase. Then, follow up with 1-3 additional emails, sent 2-5 days after their purchase, giving them best practices and pro-tips.

Here are the templates again:

Welcome Email

- **Subject Line:** [NAME], here's your access to [LOW-COST OFFER].
- Salutation with their name: "Hi [NAME]!
- **Welcome and Congratulations:** "Thank you for ordering [LOW-COST OFFER]. You made a great decision. Inside, you'll find... [BULLET POINTS WITH BENEFITS]."
- **Benefits Bullet Points:** Restate the benefits in 3-5 very brief bullet points.
- **Access Information:** If you use Kartra or ClickFunnels, the username and password to access their purchase will be the exact same username and password they need to access their Free Offer. The CRM will provide you with a merge field to give them that information here again.
- **Pro-Tip:** Give them simple instructions on the best way they can consume and put the Low-Cost Offer to use. "Your next step is to dive right in. The best way to do this is to..."
- **Call to Action:** Invite them to do something. Read a specific area in the program, check out another product, follow you on social media channels, register for a webinar, etc. Always, always, always, invite them to take action of some kind.
- **Close:** End with your unique greeting and name. I usually use something like, "To Your Best Life, Joshua".

Consumption Email

- Subject Line: Did you see [feature or benefit]?

- Salutation: "Hi [NAME]!"
- 1-3 Pro-Tips: I call them "pro-tips", but you can call them anything you'd like. Think of it like this... if you were brand-new to your world, what do you wish someone would point out or help with? Share those things with them. These suggestions can include:
    - Highlights of the best or highest-leverage areas of your Low-Cost Offer
    - Insights from other users on making the most of your offer
    - Extra tidbits that you didn't include in the core program
    - Suggestions on how to go through the Low-Cost Offer
- Call to Action: Invite them to take one specific action.
- Close: Closing salutation.

A word about your ideal buyer getting a lot of emails from you...

If you add things up, your ideal buyer is going to get a lot of emails from you. You might wonder if that is going to bother them.

The answer is NO.

When I started dating my wife, Margie, I was madly in love with her. Just about everything else on my schedule disappeared suddenly and I had time to spend with her. I WANTED to spend more and more time with her.

And that is the way humans are... when we find something we like, we focus on it. We want to devour it. We obsess over it. It fills our mind and our time... and we like it that way.

If you are selling something that solves a major challenge or fulfills a serious desire, your ideal buyer will be excited to see half a dozen emails from you in the first 10 minutes of knowing you, especially if they just invested money into learning about your solutions.

Here's a list of emails your ideal buyer will get, almost instantly, if they accept all your invitations to this point in the funnel:

- Welcome to the Family
- Free Offer Access
- Low-Cost Offer Access
- Bump Offer Access

Then, over the next few days, they will also get another 3-10 emails giving them pro-tips and best practices.

Pro Tip: One thing you can do is consider when the Consumption Emails get sent. You can intentionally stagger them.

For example, the Free Offer pro-tip email could be sent within a few hours... the Low-Cost Offer pro-tip email could be sent on day two after purchase... and the Bump Offer email could be sent on day three.

In this way, they get a helpful tip from you every day for the first week or so, without you needing to do a great deal of work.

Conclusion

Bump offers are not a new idea. In the early 70s, McDonald's realized that most of their customers only bought a hamburger.

They taught the cashiers at their 2,500 locations to ask a simple question:

"Would you like fries with that?"

On average, 50% of their customers said yes. It was a small price tag, it scratched a slightly different itch, and seemed to make sense. So, people bought. And are still buying.

Not only that, but McDonald's found people that got fries were also likely to get a drink... another profit boost.

Grocery stores have been bumping your order for way longer than McDonald's. Have you noticed how checkout lines are packed full of small, cheap, desirable, and useful items? It is so easy to toss that gum on the conveyor belt (as I found out in the checkout line with my daughter, Mary!).

When you look for it, you'll see that Bump Offers are just about everywhere. Apple wants you to add AppleCare. Southwest offers you car rentals and early bird check-in. Sam's Club self-checkout reminds you of things you've purchased before and encourages you not to forget those items. On and on it goes.

Make the decision today to add an In-Cart Bump offer to everything you sell from now until forever. You'll be so glad you did!

Action Checklist

- ☐ **1 – Define the Deliverables of Your Bump Offer –** Answer these questions: What value will I give? Why should my ideal buyer care? Why should they spend their money on this instead of a dinner and a movie (or whatever else they would drop $20 on...)?

- ☐ **2 – Create Your Bump Offer –** Bump offers should be a different product modality than the Low-Cost Offer, scratching a slightly different itch, but still within the framework of the buyer's core desire.

- ☐ **3 – Write the Bump Offer Copy –** You have less than 100 words to make the pitch and close the deal. Keep it simple and clear so it's easy to understand.

- ☐ **4 – Set Up In the CRM –** This is the same process you just went through to make your Low-Cost Offer available for purchase.

- ☐ **5 – Add the Bump Offer to the Cart –** Keep the design in harmony with your other image branding and relatable to your ideal buyer, but attention-grabbing. Be sure to place the

Bump Offer box after the contact information and order details section.

- ☐ **6 – Access and Consumption Emails –** You'll need to do this with every product you sell. Send them a brief email telling them how to access their purchase. Then, follow up with 1-3 additional emails, sent 2-5 days after their purchase, giving them best practices and pro-tips.

CHAPTER 7

Convert Small Buyers to Big Buyers

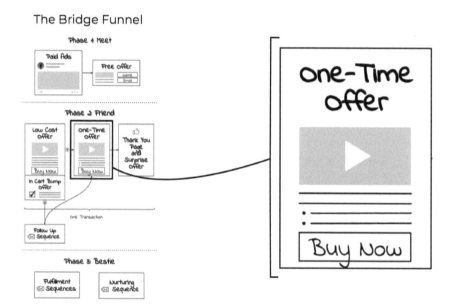

"How many times do you think we can profitably redirect them after the initial purchase and before they see the 'Thank You' Page?"

I looked up at Perry Marshall and lifted my eyebrows.

The other 12 people in the room did the same. We were all part of a top-end mastermind group of business owners.

One guy called out, "Maybe one or two? I'd think buyers would get really irritated with you after that."

A few other people threw out suggestions ranging from zero to 10.

"We recently successfully tested more than 15 post-purchase steps."

"You mean you redirected people more than 15 times before they saw the "Thank You" Page for their first purchase?" I asked. "That's insane."

"Yes, we were totally shocked. But it worked. People are far more apt to stay engaged in the purchase process than most companies think."

That was over 10 years ago. Since then, I've tested thousands of post-purchase offers. I've learned two things…

First, Perry is right. People are more than willing to engage with you for far longer than most companies believe.

Some of my clients have adamantly insisted that it would be offensive to THEIR buyers to see a One-Time Offer. And then we tested it and quadrupled their average transaction.

I've tested this with SaaS, B2B, health and fitness, cosmetics and skin care, financial newsletters, training courses, emergency preparedness products, jewelry, non-profit fundraising, and hundreds of other industries, products, and services.

If someone loves you enough to buy from you once, they love you enough to buy from you twice, thrice, quadrice (yes, that's a real, unofficial word, but I like it!), and more.

As marketing legend, Dan Kennedy, says, "A buyer is a buyer is a buyer".

And do you remember the old expression, "Strike while the iron is hot"? It applies here. The best time for someone to buy more things from you is right when they buy things from you.

If you are not aggressively and strategically using one-click offers, you are likely losing at least half the revenues you could be making…

and more likely, you're losing three or four times the revenue you could have.

As my friend and mentor, RC Peck, said to me once, "Joshua, it's like you're in a huge room with a massive pile of gold in the middle of the room. You just keep walking around it but never reach out and grab it. Stop walking around it and start putting the gold in your pocket!"

The One-Time Offer is positioned immediately after the Low-Cost Offer. Instead of sending them to the "Thank You" Page, you direct them to another offer page.

We are NOT going to create 15 different redirects and offers. For the purposes of this book, we will focus on creating a single One-Time Offer, specifically an Upsell.

But I will briefly explain to you the different kinds of One-Time Offers you can make.

As you read these, keep in mind that you need to make them an offer that is a different category than what they have already purchased. It can be a different topic or a different product type. Stay one step ahead of them on their Transformational Journey and keep scratching unique itches.

Upsell and Downsell One-Click Offers

We call this a One-Time Offer because you will make them an incredible deal that will show up only in connection with the funnel they are currently in. If they don't buy it now, at this price, they will lose their chance.

The only exception to this is if you implement a follow-up sequence similar to the one you created for the Low-Cost Offer. In that case, you will send them back to this offer page.

This is a very important point that I learned from Brendon Burchard... have integrity in your marketing.

If you have a deadline, keep the deadline. If you say it's a One-Time Offer only available on a specific page, only make it available on that page. If you say there are limited seats or quantity of something, be truthful about those numbers.

This builds trust because, over time, people will know if you're telling the truth or not.

If you lie about things like this, it is like the old story of "The Boy Who Cried Wolf!"... pretty soon, no one will believe you and your funnels will be flat and lack serious conversions... especially when marketing to your best customers, your existing buyers.

Kartra, ClickFunnels, and other CRMs make it fairly easy to do this. You can have each person on their own deadlines and offers that expire in a timeframe relative to them.

For example, when an ideal buyer sees an offer that expires in 24 hours, the system tracks that individual buyer and expires the offer right on time. You might have 1,000 buyers on a specific deadline or seeing a specific offer... and it could be a different deadline date for all of them.

When you set up your system right, it is like you're having a private, one-on-one conversation with each individual ideal buyer. To me, it is one of the most incredible aspects of modern marketing technology. It allows you to custom-tailor experiences for your audience and really connect with them in ways that are not possible in a static, mass-marketing world.

Here are the three types of One-Time Offers:

> **Upsell** – You offer them something more expensive than what they just bought.
>
> **Downsell** – This is an offer less expensive than the Upsell. Note that I did not say it was the same price as the Low-Cost Offer. It is a downsell from the price point of the Upsell.

Neutral Sell – When your list is sensitive to costs or has been trained to buy within a specific price range, you should make them an offer that is close to the price of the Low-Cost Offer.

You should only use this at the end of a complex funnel sequence or if you have proven, long-term data on your ideal buyer's price thresholds.

If you were building out a more complicated funnel, you would have all three One-Time Offers ready to deploy. In just a minute, I'll show you how it all flows together.

How to Position Your One-Time Offer

If you position your One-Time Offer correctly—meaning the tone and approach feels like you're giving them a gift instead of bleeding them for more money—they will admire and appreciate you. They will trust you more and want to stay connected to you.

A key point here is to ensure that your One-Time Offer is valuable to them and in line with their Transformational Journey. Are you "building a bridge" for them or fleecing them for stuff they don't really want or need?

They will know the difference and so will you.

One-Click Offer Pricing Principles

Because you are making an offer that requires very little education and information... and that has a problem/solution argument that is very well known to the buyer... the main place where you can lose the sale is in the price.

You will set the price at $37 for now with a retail price of around $299 (89% discount). Of course, you can play around with these price points, depending on what you're offering, but these are time-tested price ranges.

As you can see, you should always calculate two different prices.

First, the retail price. This is the actual price of the offer, including all the value it brings. Think of this as the sticker price on a car or the price before discounts, special offers, promotions, etc.

This price should be as large as you can honestly and realistically make it. Never overinflate or hype up a price. Buyers sense fake stuff a mile away. But also, don't shy away from setting a respectable fair market value.

The second price to set is the Offer Price. This is the price the buyer will actually pay. In most cases, if you are a Price Simplifier, you should give them a discount off the Retail Price of between 50% and 90%.

If, for some reason, you can't make the price points of $299 retail price and $37 Offer Price work, then recalculate using these principles:

- A One-Time Offer Upsell should have an Offer Price of around 5x the price of your initial offer. If you sold them something for $7, then you should put the end price at around $35. If you sold something for $1000, then you can go as high as $5,000.
- The Retail Price should be 4x to 10x that number to make it a real discount. Again, never falsely inflate your retail price. Focus on creating real value and then offer them a legitimate discount and Offer Price. Remember, this is a One-Time Offer that will never be offered anywhere else.

CONVERT SMALL BUYERS TO BIG BUYERS

TO PREVENT DOUBLE CHARGES, DO NOT PRESS BACK, RELOAD, OR CLOSE THIS PAGE
I <u>Really</u> Want You To Have This Training... ← *Eyebrow*

GROUND-BREAKING NEW TRAINING

Headline →
All Of Your Ideal Clients Are On LinkedIn. Here's How To Get Them With Your <u>Perfect Article</u>...

Deck Copy → *Grab My World-Class LinkedIn Magic Formula To Get Writing Projects... Today!*

← *Video*

Call to Action →
Yes! Upgrade My Order!
Clicking Here Will Charge Your Card Just $47 :)

No Thanks, I Don't Want LinkedIn Magic Right Now... I Can Get Clients By Myself

All My Wealthiest Students Use This!

← *Product Box Shots*

Offer Details →

✓ **LinkedIn Magic Masterclass** - Some parts of this program are very visual. I will show you exactly what to do so that there is no guesswork. Each video is short - no more than 20 minutes so that you can get all my secrets in as little time as possible. Plus, it is designed to be consumed over time so that you don't get overwhelmed. The videos can be played online or downloaded to your mobile device for viewing and reviewing anywhere, anytime. $397 Value!

✓ **Complete MP3 Files** - You will also receive complete MP3 files taken from the videos. This way you can listen to them on the go.

✓ **Templates and Scripts** - All of the trainings come with templates and scripts. Fill in the blanks and start TODAY!

✓ **Guidebook and Worksheets** - You'll receive a simple, clear guidebooks and worksheets. These will guide you through each step and help you know exactly what to do next.

✓ **Community Support** - We've created a Facebook page where you can connect with your friends and fellow students. You will get the support, answers, and insights you need to succeed!

✓ **BONUS: Content Calendar Tool - $97 Value!**

Creating Your One-Time Offer

The process to create your One-Time Offer is much the same as the creation of the Free Offer, the Low-Cost Offer, and the Bump Offer.

There is a secret to creating this offer that many people overlook...

You have done a great deal of research and creative thinking, designing, and publishing. You have thought through different product types using the Unlimited Offer System with the seven offer categories.

You have been building bridges and thinking deeply about your ideal buyer's Transformational Journey. You have solutions and ways to realize deep desires.

But, you have put everything into a small package so far.

At this point, you have everything you need for a much bigger, more in-depth offering.

Here are a few ideas of what you could do with everything you have so far:

Complete Focused Course

This will not be your flagship offer, but close. Your flagship course usually contains everything someone needs to complete the full journey. It brings massive tools, insights, and resources to the table.

So, hold off on creating that right now... and know that everything you've done so far and will do in the future will help you create a beautiful, amazing flagship offer.

But for now, you can take one of the most critical steps and really go deep.

For example, I first met Perry Marshall because I wanted to figure out how to do Google Ads. He had a free seven-day mini-course on online marketing.

That was followed by his best-selling book, "The Definitive Guide to Google Adwords", which sold for around $20... but he ran specials where you could get it for $0.01 if you just paid shipping of $9.95.

Then he offered a program called Adwords Copywriting Express that retailed for $497... but you could pick it up for just $69 if you gave his newsletter a try.

The Adwords Copywriting Express course takes one section of the journey—namely writing ads and promotional copy—and goes incredibly deep and detailed.

This is an excellent format option for your One-Time Offer. What aspect of the ideal buyer's Transformational Journey are you extremely good at? What idea or concept could you go very deep on... in your sleep?

Map out the steps within that step to help your ideal buyer quickly achieve incredible results and master. Then write out the system... or record it... or video yourself talking about it. I have seen experts simply have someone interview them with pre-set questions and video-record it. The video, audio, and transcripts get sold in all kinds of places, including as a One-Time Offer.

Repurpose Existing Materials

If you have a recording of you speaking, doing a webinar or live seminar, past articles and essays, training modules, etc.

And material that you've created in the past can work great for a One-Time Offer.

Gary Halbert was one of the best copywriters in the world. He wrote a series of letters to his son about copywriting and marketing. Later, those letters were edited and turned into a book and then a training program.

Anthony Robbins turns his live events into digital productions and resells them—usually making more on the digital products than he did on the live event. Plus, the content is turned into books, audio programs, podcasts, etc.

A financial advisor I know takes his 10 best podcasts and sells them as a mini-course.

My point is this… if you have content already created, you can repackage and repurpose it as a One-Time Offer.

Bundle Offers

Similar to repurposing existing content and turning it into a new offer, you can take courses, books, programs, etc., and offer them in a bundle at a huge discount.

Brendon Burchard has done this many times. For a long time, he offered a "Confidence Course"… a bundle of a few mini-course he'd created that related to building confidence.

Maybe you don't need to create a new offer… just bundle stuff you already have and sell that.

New Material

Of course, you always have the option of creating brand-new material. For example, if you know that a critical step in the transformation journey is coming up, and you don't have any materials to address it, you can create it.

Think of something that would bring at least $300 in value and put it together using the suggestions and ideas we talked about previously.

Here are the steps you need to take to create your One-Time Offer.

1 – Define the One-Time Offer Deliverables

Using the same principles and workflow you used to create your other offers, define a clear deliverable for this offer.

If you are repurposing or bundling your materials, look at the whole picture. When they use these various tools and resources, what will they get? How will this help them come closer to fulfilling their desires?

2 – Create the Offer

Again, you will use the exact same process and steps to create this offer as you have with the others.

By now, you should begin to feel a distinct rhythm and flow to the process. Non-negotiable appointments with yourself... choose the format... write the outline... write, create, and record... polish and format, etc.

A word of caution at this point... remember the Bob Iger quote about innovate or die?

Innovation does not come in the process I've outlined. Meaning, use the principles for creation that we've discussed. You'll have your own unique style and focus, but I've identified core principles that universally apply.

The innovation comes in one of two forms—the actual offer you're making or the format you're delivering that offer in.

Your solutions and how you help the ideal buyer fulfill their deep desires can be revolutionary and innovative. And, you can choose to give that to them in a course, video, in person, virtually, in an app, etc., or a combination of all of the above.

I know some companies, for their virtual events, send their ideal buyers physical event packages that include guidebooks, popcorn, restaurant gift cards, books, and other things that relate to the presentation.

I'm going to tell you something that will sound like I'm contradicting myself, but it is a very important point to remember at this point...

Mark Ford once told me that creativity and innovation were highly overrated.

In effect, he told me, "I've made most of my money replicating things that have already been successful. I just add my own style and approach and sell it."

For example, he has made a fortune in financial newsletters. He did not invent the financial newsletters. He just produces them with excellence. Same with investing in rare and unique art. He didn't invent art, he just sells it. Real Estate... same thing.

Yes, it is important to be innovative. And sometimes that innovation simply comes in the form of adding your own unique style and approach to proven, time-tested ideas. Steve Jobs did not invent the MP3 player. He just made it easier to use in the form of the iPod and marketed it with excellence.

I think of it like this... I have two choices:

- **Revolutionary** – I can be a pioneer and innovate something totally new and creative. This requires me to spend a great deal of time and money on R&D, educating the buyer, and breaking into or creating new markets. Sometimes this is needed and I'm grateful for the people that do this.
- **Evolutionary** – I can see what is already working, what is proven, and put my own unique spin on it or find the flaws and improve it. In this case, I capitalize on existing marketing. I spend less on educating my ideal buyer. Like Sir Isaac Newton says, I can stand on the shoulders of the giants that have gone before me.
- Both paths work. At this stage of the game, I highly recommend you see yourself as an evolutionary creator. Let's get something created, out the door, selling, and making you money before you tackle those revolutionary ideas you may have.

3 – Write the Sales Copy

Follow the sales page templates outlined in the other offers.

As a reminder, this copy needs to be short. The video script should be short, 3-10 minutes. At this point, they are still right in the middle of their initial buying experience with you. This is another impulse buy. It is another step on their journey. Make it exciting, rewarding, and easy for them to take!

Shoot the Video

Just like with your Low-Cost Offer, you'll find that a short, simple sales video will greatly increase your conversion rates on this page.

Grab your smartphone and just do it following the scripts I've given you.

4 – Set Up the Product in Your CRM

Set this up according to the process in your CRM. Set up automations so that when they buy, this gets added to their membership/library area. Nothing sparks customer service complaints faster than buying an offer that they don't actually get!

5 – Create the Sales Page and Order Page

Once you have sales copy, video, and the product setup in your CRM, you can assemble everything.

The layout for your Sales Page and Order Page for this will be exactly the same as your Low-Cost Offer.

Change up the colors and copy on the page just enough so that your ideal buyer knows that this is a different page. You don't want them thinking, "Oh, I've already seen this page!"

A simple way to do this is to be sure to have different clothes on and use a different background for your sales video. Also, you can change up the color of your Eyebrow Copy or the background colors.

6 – Write Access and Consumption Emails

Even though their username and email address are the same, you still need to send them a note that confirms their purchase and tells them how to access the offer. Use the templates I gave you for the other offers.

Same thing applies for the Consumption Emails… but, you should consider writing a few more emails for this offer.

Your One-Time Offer should be bigger, provide more details, and be a little more involved and comprehensive than your other offers. Because of this, it might be useful for the ideal buyer to have 3-10 pro-tip emails that help them consume this offer.

You are building a long-term relationship and trust here. An ideal buyer that feels recognized and supported will come back time and time again to buy from you. It is worth your time and effort to write a couple more emails to help them succeed.

7 – Set Up the Emails in the CRM

Add your emails to the CRM and automate them. The Access Email will go out immediately after purchase. The others can be staggered over the course of a week or two.

Again, with a little planning, you can have these go out on different days than the pro-tip emails from the other offers they've just purchased. Spread them out. Maximize your communication opportunities with your ideal buyer. 10 emails over a three-week period is way better than 10 emails in 30 seconds.

Conclusion

Alwin had a growth challenge. He sold software and was really good at selling it... but, at the end of the day, he really only had one offer.

"Alwin, we need a One-Time Offer to increase the value you're giving to your buyers and increase their Lifetime Customer Value to you."

We brainstormed together and thought of what could make life easier for them.

"What really drives your buyers crazy and costs them a lot of time?"

Alwin's company, Collectorz, specializes in organizing collections. DVD and video collections. LP record collections. Book collections. Comic collections. Etc.

"Data input is by far the hardest part for them," he said.

"Ok. Can we find a way to sell them a barcode scanner? They can point and click and have all the info they need, right?"

Alwin agreed and went to work finding a barcode scanner that he could source for cheap and sell at a nice profit margin. He found a little device called the CueCat... a little barcode scanner that looked like a mouse. It was originally designed to only scan a specific barcode, but when the company failed, they needed to liquidate inventory. With a little software tweak, the scanner could now read any barcode, making it perfect for Collectorz customers.

We added it as a One-Time Offer, with a profit margin of around $30. Thousands of customers bought the scanner, saving them untold hours of keying in barcode information... and making Collectorz an incredible profit.

Action Checklist

- [ ] **1 – Define the One-Time Offer Deliverables** – Using the same principles and workflow you used to create your other offers, define a clear deliverable for this offer.

- [ ] **2 – Create the Offer** – Again, you will use the exact same process and steps to create this offer as you have with the others. By now, you should begin to feel a distinct rhythm and flow to this process. Non-negotiable appointments with yourself... choose the format... write the outline... write, create, and record... polish and format, etc.

- [ ] **3 – Write the Sales Copy** – Follow the sales page templates outlined in the other offers. As a reminder, this copy needs to be short.

- [ ] **4 – Set Up the Product in Your CRM** – Set this up according to the process in your CRM. Set up automations so that when they buy, this gets added to their membership/library area.

- [ ] **5 – Create the Sales Page and Order Page** – The layout for your Sales Page and Order Page for this will be exactly the same as your Low-Cost Offer. Change up the colors and copy on the page just enough so that your ideal buyer knows that this is a different page.

- [ ] **6 – Write Access and Consumption Emails** – As always, send them an email telling them how to access their purchase. Consider writing a few more Consumption Emails (2-5) for this offer, depending on how detailed it is. Remember, you're building a long-term relationship here.

- [ ] **7 – Set Up the Emails in the CRM** – Add your emails to the CRM and automate them.

CHAPTER 8

Turn "Thank You" Into Income

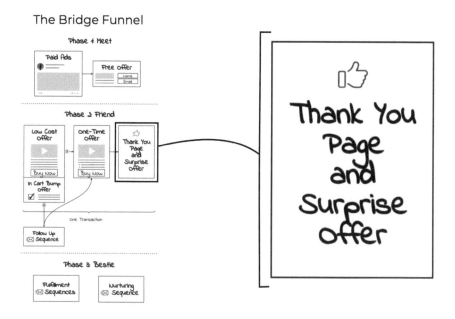

When my wife was a little girl, she was in a singing group called Erms Worms. Her aunt, Erma, organized and conducted the group of young singers.

They traveled around to nursing homes and other community activities singing old songs and bringing joy to people.

One of my favorite songs went something like this...

> There are two little magic words that will open any door with ease. One little word is, "Thanks!" And the other little word is, "Please!"

Nothing is truer in marketing than the power of asking politely for a sale... and showing deep, genuine gratitude when it comes.

I discovered the power of expressing appreciation and asking for the sale in 2002 when I was working as the finance director on a US Senate campaign.

Secrets Learned on a Montana US Senate Campaign

One day, I was sitting thinking about how I could increase donations. The thought came to me... "Joshua, you need to express more gratitude to your donors. When you do, they will feel appreciation and they will feel recognized. They will want to give more, so in the act of thanking them, make it easy for them to give more."

If that sounds like a greedy, capitalistic approach to gratitude, maybe it is. But, I couldn't help remembering the principle that Charlie "Tremendous" Jones taught me... if people don't buy from you, they don't value what you have to offer and you can't change their life.

In politics, the more someone donates, the more likely they are to vote, encourage others to vote, and uphold the values they voted for. Yes, we needed the money, but the voters also needed a boost in patriotism and political activism. That is, after all, the core foundation of our Democratic-Republic.

I sat down with the candidate and, together, we wrote up a sincere "Thank You" note. It included this postscript.

> "P.S. I'm sure you agree that winning this election is critical to Montana and the United States. Will you please take a minute to pass along the enclosed donation envelope to someone you know? We would love their support to win this election!"

Then, we included a donation envelope along with a short note for the donor's friend or family member.

I also coded those envelopes so we could track how effective our efforts were. We did the same things with online donations and email replies.

The result was astonishing! We discovered that most people didn't pass along their envelope... they simply sent back another donation of their own. In effect, in a relatively short time, we almost doubled our donations simply by saying "please" and "thank you".

It Worked for a SaaS Company, Too!

More than 10 years later, I did something similar with a large SaaS company. Instead of asking new buyers and people who communicated with Customer Service to fill out a survey or give a testimonial, we sent them a private discount code with this message:

> "I want to personally thank you for contacting our Customer Service team. We love helping you and hope everything was resolved.
>
> To show how much we appreciate you being part of our family, I'm giving you a private discount code that gives you 20% off any purchase or upgrade.
>
> Will you please pass this on to someone you know could use our software? (Or, feel free to use it yourself!)

Thanks again for being a loyal customer. Just hit reply if you need anything else!"

This instantly turned customer service into a profit center and increased new customer value by over 30%.

So, how can you use these "two little magic words" in your funnel?

One of the most powerful ways to do this is with a strategically crafted "Thank You" Page.

This comes at the end of Phase Two of the funnel, after you have invited them to accept your Free Offer, Low-Cost Offer, Bump Offer, and One-Time Offer.

As mentioned earlier, at any point where they do not accept one of the offers, you pull them out of the funnel and show them the "Thank You" Page. This shows them that you respect their decision. It honors their "no" and allows them to stay in control of the conversation.

Your ideal buyer will appreciate this and respect you for it. Our testing and studies show that this increases long-term sales and Lifetime Customer Value. You don't need to press them hard on the first day... you're building a long-term relationship and will have many, many opportunities to sell them things in the future.

The "Thank You" Page plays two roles:

First, it is a deep, sincere, and warm message of appreciation.

This is not an ulterior motive, sneaky message to trick them into buying more or liking you.

This is you, looking them in the eyes, and sincerely expressing gratitude. Our ideal buyers are the reason we are in business. We should admire, love, respect, and appreciate them.

I was once in a mastermind meeting with half a dozen influencers and entrepreneurs. One of them said, "I love what I do, but newbies are so clueless. They ask the same stupid questions over and over again and waste my team's time. It drives me crazy."

The moderator of the group looked a little shocked and saddened by the comment. He said, "If you don't learn to love so-called newbies, you'll never grow. These people are the lifeblood of your business. Their growth and transformation should be your mission and love. You should honor them for trying and reaching for a better life."

I fully agree with that position and suggest you take on the same belief. New people are the lifeblood of your business. Find joy in serving them, helping them, and showing them deep appreciation.

The second purpose of the "Thank You" Page is to serve as a bridge between the worlds of your ideal buyer being a new friend or acquaintance and being your BEST friend who is excited to go on a journey with you for many years to come.

In other words, the "Thank You" Page serves to invite your ideal buyer to go deeper into your world.

To create a powerful "Thank You" Page that creates strong loyalty and becomes a profit center for you, use these key elements:

- **Eyebrow Copy** – At the very top of the page, confirm that you received their order and are sending it ASAP. "Thank you! We got your order and it is on its way!"
- **Headline Copy** – A large "Thank You" and an expression of appreciation.
- **Image** – Have the image right next to the headline. The best image is of a person—Influencer, Founder, CEO, etc.—that has weight in the buyer's life. What I mean is, if I see a person on the "Thank You" Page that I don't know, it has less impact than if I see a picture of and get a message from the influencer I just bought from... or the person who developed the system I just bought... etc. We all love attention from the top players.
- **Video Script** – This is a short video. 3-5 minutes. If you do a video (and I recommend you do!), it should follow this simple template:

- **Congratulations** – Congratulate them on making a great choice and joining your business family.
- **Gratitude** – Express sincere appreciation for them and their purchase. I like to spend a minute deeply thinking about their real lives, all the things they could spend money on, the challenges they likely face, and how they honored me by choosing to be part of my world. It is an act of trust and a vote of confidence. When I see my ideal buyer in my mind, it is easy to tell them how much I truly appreciate them (and if you're reading this, that includes you! Thank you!).
- **Unannounced Bonus** – Let them know you have an unannounced gift for them. (See below for details on what this gift or bonus could be…)
- **Social Proof** – Tell them a story about someone in your world and the results of their Transformational Journey with you. This could be your own story.
- **Free Bonus Details** – Outline what you're giving them.
- **Call to Action** – Invite them to click on the big button to accept the Free Offer.
- **More Gratitude** – End with another expression of gratitude and appreciation for them and their purchase.

- **Record the Video** – Just like with the Order Upsell pages, videos convert the best here. With a video, people can see your facial expressions, hear the tone of your voice, and really feel your gratitude and appreciation.
- **"Thank You" Page Copy** – Under the video, write a short paragraph thanking them and telling them similar things as you put in the video. You should use short bullet point statements to detail their free gift.

- **Create the Page in the CRM** – Your CRM will have a template you can use. It should include these elements, in this order:
  - Eyebrow Copy
  - Headline Copy
  - Video
  - Sub-Head
  - Body Copy
  - Large Call to Action Button (i.e. "Yes! I Accept Your Free Gift")
  - Social Proof Elements
- **Set Up Automations** – The "Thank You" Page will be the trigger for a series of automations.

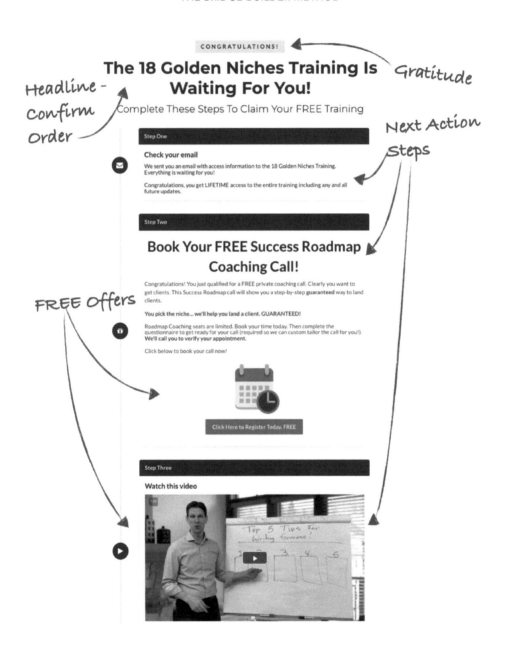

"Thank You" Page Offers

There are a number of things you can offer on your "Thank You" Page.

There are a few key things to consider when creating this offer…

Simple

This does not have to be something grand. Of course, if you have something mind-blowing and amazing, definitely offer it. But if you don't, this can be very, very simple.

Here are a few ideas to consider:

- **Existing Content** – You can give your ideal buyer access to an existing article, podcast, or video. You can bundle a few related items and give them the bundle. I've done this with articles that I did in a three or four-part series.
- **Physical Gift** – There is something wonderful about getting a book, pens, or a sample in the mail. People don't mind paying a small shipping fee for free physical gifts. I've seen people give away free guidebooks, travel guides, books, and other goodies, and the buyer pays a small $7 fee for shipping.
- **Webinar** – If you have good ideas and are comfortable with live presentations or PowerPoint slides, this is a great option for you. Think of one core idea from your journey that you can teach on, create an outline, and book a time to present it to your ideal buyers. The best part is, it doesn't really matter if you have 20,000 people show up or no one shows up, you can record it and reuse it in the future for a variety of different things. See the Bonus Page for a complete template on how to organize and run an effective webinar.
- **Small Group Coaching** – Another great idea if you have something to teach or train on as a coach or mentor. Simply set

a time, run the group coaching session, record it, and reuse it. If you are just starting out, you can invite a handful of people to do a coaching session with you for free.

- **Private Analysis and Roadmap** – This can be a little more time-consuming. If you are selling a high-end offer down the road, this is a great option. Create a questionnaire and invite your ideal buyer to complete the questionnaire and then book a private analysis and roadmap session with you. For example, the questionnaire might ask them about their most pressing challenge (great market research). Have them provide examples such as copy, website, health stats, or whatever is relevant to your industry. Analyze it and then jump on the phone and help them create a roadmap for their Transformational Journey. This obviously can lead to bigger consulting and coaching proposals.
- **Test Drive/Trial Subscription** – If you have a membership, software, or a community, give them unfettered access for 7-14 days. Surprise them with an experience of being inside your world. If they love it, they just might stick around.
- **Interviews** – If you have done (or are willing to do) interviews, you can offer recordings of these interviews as a free gift. Alternatively, you can invite your ideal buyer to do an interview with you. This allows them to have a voice, helps you connect with them, provides excellent research data for you, and gives you long-term content you can use again and again.

Bridge Experience

The "Thank You" Page Offer is a Bridge. They have just accepted one or more of your offers. You're now inviting them to come deeper into your world as an honored guest.

Make sure that whatever you offer them right here both provides value to them and brings them further into your world. You'll notice that all of the ideas I listed above do exactly that.

Free Gift – Not Another Pitch

There is some debate on this… should you make one last offer to them? Or should you give them a goodwill gift?

I've seen the funnel data on some of the most successful marketers in the world. "Thank You" Page paid offers tend to convert at around 1%-3%. It is not much.

By contrast, free "Thank You" gifts tend to convert as high as 40%. When people accept your Free Offer, they are making one more micro-commitment.

Additionally, you are invoking the persuasion law of "Commitment and Consistency", making this a "salt the oats" experience instead of making it feel like you're trying to squeeze just a few more pennies out of them. Paid offers tend to make the appreciation feel less sincere and defeat the purpose of having this page.

On top of all that, people that accept a free "Thank You" Page offer are 80% more likely to buy something in your next promotion. It is a very valuable investment.

Clear Problem/Solution Offer

As with the other offers, make sure that the problem/solution equation is crystal clear. Know that the next step is what they need and offer it to them.

How to Frame Your "Thank You" Page Offer

THE BRIDGE BUILDER METHOD

Years ago, I was commissioned by B&B Electronics to write one whitepaper a month for them. B&B Electronics serviced the manufacturing and energy industries by creating custom hardware and electrical solutions for them.

Traditionally, a whitepaper is a boring, dry, technical document. It is not usually seen as overly valuable or what you would call a "persuasion hit piece"!

B&B was hopeful that I could change that around for them. They wanted their whitepapers to be used as lead-generation tools to get the phones ringing.

I studied what they had done before. Sure enough, dry, boring, data-driven documents. I did two things:

First, I added stories to illustrate the point and give some color to the whitepaper.

Second, I added a small call to action at the end.

I invited them to meet with one of the B&B Electronics engineers for a free consultation and design session. I detailed the credentials of the engineers. I then explained that normally a design session with this level of engineer would cost several thousand dollars... but they could get a free 30-minute session if they filled out a simple form and booked the call.

This is a version of what I call the "Tom Sawyer Effect". Do you remember in the beginning of the book where Tom has to whitewash the fence—a task he hates? He comes up with an idea to make it look like whitewashing the fence is the most exciting, most coveted activity in the little town of St. Petersburg, MO.

Pretty soon, instead of Tom whitewashing the fence, he has half a dozen of his buddies doing all the work for him and paying him for the "privilege" of doing it.

Tom took something mundane and built value around it. You might argue that Tom swindled those poor boys... but in reality, he gave them a gift—the gift of work and the joy of making something beautiful. Tom's Aunt Polly didn't see it that way, but it is a true perspective.

I did the same with the engineers at B&B Technology... what was presented as a sales pitch, something nobody likes, was turned into an invaluable consulting session with top engineers.

It worked and they used that series of whitepapers for more than a decade.

Conclusion and Summary

The car slowly pulled to a stop. Looking out the window, I gasped and turned to Margie.

Her eyes were filled with wonder as well.

The home we just stopped in front of was a massive contemporary-style mansion. My initial guess was that it was over 15,000 square feet. The grounds were filled with flowers and shrubs that looked like they belonged in a king's palace.

Every detail was perfect. It was so beautiful and fit so well into the surroundings that it took your breath away.

Margie and I were guests at this home, belonging to the CEO of one of the largest gift companies in the world, who I'll call Tim.

Tim had just developed a new personal development model, not related to his gift company, but something he and his wife, Lori, were very passionate about. I was hired as the marketing consultant and copywriter to help him launch the brand and spread it around the world.

We were there for a three-day mastermind session with the other consultants and partners. Tim and Lori had graciously invited Margie to come and be their guest and spend time with Lori while Tim and I talked shop.

Getting out of the car, I took Margie's hand and felt her give me a tight squeeze. We had never associated with wealthy people at this level.

It was a little intimidating. I had never met Tim or Lori and didn't know exactly what to expect.

As we approached the door—two massive frosted glass doors ornately etched with flowers and trees—the doors slid open. Tim and Lori literally bounded out of the house and down the stairs.

Without any pretenses or introduction, Tim threw his arms around me and embraced me like we had been best friends for decades. Lori did the same with Margie... and then they swapped and I got a huge, warm hug from Lori while Tim embraced Margie.

With his arm still around Margie, Tim reached out and took my hand, "Joshua, I'm so grateful you're here! Seriously, bro, thanks for coming to our home! We are truly honored!"

Lori gave us a glowing smile and squeezed my shoulder again. "Yes, Margie, I can't wait to spend time with you. It is a rare treat to meet someone with so many beautiful children. What a joy to have you here!"

The welcome was so sincere and the appreciation was so palpable that it brought tears to my eyes. I felt instant trust and loyalty for this wonderful couple. Whatever they were doing, I was all in.

When you create your "Thank You" Page, I want you to remember this greeting and the warmth, love, and appreciation we felt. When you can come close to replicating that, you'll discover that your ideal buyer will reflect those feelings back to you.

One last song from Margie's childhood singing group. This one is called "The Magic Penny", by Malvina Reynolds:

> Love is something if you give it away,
> Give it away, give it away.
> Love is something if you give it away,
> You end up having more.
> It's just like a magic penny,
> Hold it tight and you won't have any.

Lend it, spend it, and you'll have so many
They'll roll all over the floor.

When you treat your ideal buyer with love, respect, and appreciation, they will feel it and your pennies will multiply.

Summary and Key Principles

- **Simple** – Your "Thank You" Page offer doesn't need to be something grand. What do you have available that you can repurpose? What is the next phase of your buyer's Transformational Journey?
- **Bridge Experience** – The "Thank You" Page should help move them into the next phase of their journey with you. What do they need to know?
- **Free Gift** – Not Another Pitch—if the "Thank You" Page is actually a "Thank You, and I want more of your money" page, it will be much less effective.
- **Clear Problem/Solution Offer** – This goes back to how well you know your customer's Transformational Journey. What simple problem can you help solve for them? If they can tell you really understand and relate to them, this page will build amazing trust.
- **Make it Very Valuable** – The way you present your offer on this page should make people feel like they're getting an incredible gift. It needs to be super valuable and be presented as such.

Phase Three: Bestie

"Joshua, the problem is this: We have a global relaunch of two products and the release of a totally new product... but our list has not been responding lately. Open rates are low and sales are flat."

I nodded, knowing exactly what Bernie was talking about.

"Bernie, I reviewed your emails and think I know what the trouble is and how to fix it. How would you classify the tone and approach of your emails to your customers?" I asked.

Bernie thought about that for a minute.

"Ads... trying to get them to buy more stuff from us."

"That's fair. After reading over 100 of your past emails, I'd agree with that. Now, let me ask you this, do you have any friends? I mean, really good friends that you really respect and admire and love being around? You know... as my children say, 'Besties'?"

Bernie laughed, "Yeah. But what's your point?"

"Every time they're around you, do they ask you for something—especially money?"

Bernie stopped laughing. "I think I see your point. You're saying that every time we email our customers, the only thing we do is ask for money, right? And that isn't great for the relationship. I think if I had a friend like that, I'd avoid spending time with them."

I nodded. "Exactly. Think of how many bad jokes there are about that weird relative that only comes around when they need money. It is just tackless and hurts relationships in real life. Well, it does the same thing in email. That's because email is real life. It is a real conversation. Your customers see it much like sitting down with you personally and having a chat."

"So, how do we fix it?" Bernie asked.

The answer to that question is the purpose of this phase of the funnel.

I cannot emphasize enough this key idea:

"The best marketing and sales strategy is a one-on-one, personal conversation with another human being."

All the pages, emails, videos, posts, etc., and the strategies we use to fill those communication channels... are nothing more than private conversations with another human being.

Yes, we send these messages out to the masses. Yes, we want the masses to buy from us. Yes, we want an ever-expanding sphere of influence.

But, in the end, what we are really doing is building a relationship. A friendship. We are finding best friends that want to listen to us, be around us, and be loyal to us for years and years to come.

And we want to be around them!

Phase Three is all about building that mutually-beneficial relationship. It is all about creating emotional connective tissue. It is all about nurturing the friendship so that you feel like you're "besties" with your ideal buyers... and they feel the same way about you.

Your primary conversation tool is email, with video as a secondary channel.

When you see your emails in this light, the strategy I show you in this section becomes natural. It flows because you stop thinking about how you can squeeze another penny out of your ideal buyer and you start thinking about how to build a life-long "bestie" friendship.

True friendships come naturally to us. We know that they are based on mutual trust, respect, and value exchange.

Your part is to serve them. Anticipate the steps of their Journey. Give them important value to help them along their way. Entertain, encourage, and embrace them through stories.

And, invite them to invest in their journey and take action. True friends challenge us to be better, don't they? Yes, and we love them all the more for it.

The ideal buyer's role in all of this is to reciprocate all of your efforts by expressing appreciation in the form of testimonials and public posts. And, of course, to buy... the surest sign of their support and friendship with you.

Let's put a framework on how to use email to build this life-long bestie relationship...

CHAPTER 9

The Hands-Free Wealth Formula

The Bridge Funnel

Tears streamed down my little 10-year-old face as I pulled my grandma's quilt up closer to my face and blew my nose in it.

February 28, 1983, I joined more than 106 million viewers to see the final episode of the hit TV series of M*A*S*H.

The first episode of M*A*S*H aired when I was a six-month embryo inside my mother, Kristine's tummy. From my youngest years, I remember sitting with my sister, Ruth, watching M*A*S*H.

Week in and week out, we cleared our schedule to sit down together after dinner and watch Hawkey and Radar and Margaret and all the others live their lives out on a fictitious battlefield in Vietnam.

My grandma, Jeanine, invited all of us to come to her house to watch the final episode. She made us popcorn and had a huge bowl of candy waiting for us. We ate it all. Laughed. Cried.

As the larger-than-life word "Goodbye" was shown painted on the rocks as Hawkey flew away, I ran to my sister, Ruth, and hugged her tight and cried and cried.

Why? What was it that drew us in each week and compelled us to spend so much devoted time and energy to this TV series?

And, how can you replicate this kind of powerful devotion and loyalty in your relationship with your ideal buyer?

The core secret lies in creating a full and complete set of connective emotions with your ideal buyer.

I loved watching M*A*S*H because, in less than 26 minutes, I knew I was going to laugh... and feel stress... and experience conflict... and go through the mundane... and sit on the edge of my seat with suspense... and get away with a little rebellion... and cry with sorrow and then cry with joy.

It was the full range of emotions and experiences that make humans... humans.

Also notice that, like most TV series of the time, the program was interrupted every 7-10 minutes to show 2-3 commercials selling me stuff.

On average, commercials consumed about 17% of the viewing time of M*A*S*H.

Or, to put it another way, 26 minutes of entertainment with about 4.5 minutes of commercials. That's 5.77 :1.

Look at that ratio again.

The entertainment input... the emotional input... the drama input... the value input... far exceeds the advertisement input.

With this number in mind, think of someone in your life that is a "bestie"... someone you spend a great deal of time with.

What is the ratio between how much you spend with them "connecting" versus how much time you spend asking them for something or calling in a favor?

It is clear to see that you spend most of your time in connection mode and little time in request mode, right?

Your email relationship needs to be structured the same way with your ideal buyer.

To make it easy to remember, I set the ratio at 80/20... about 80% of your emails should be written to connect with and give value to your ideal buyer. 20% will invite them to take action, usually to buy something.

This 80/20 ratio gives a cyclical rhythm to your communications.

Here's a framework for the pattern, The Nurturing Sequence. After I outline this framework, we'll look at creating your Flagship Offer and show you how to use these emails to sell it.

Each cycle will have about 11 emails. Before I outline the framework, let me give you a few definitions and key concepts...

Value Emails

I define a "value" email as anything that improves the quality of life for my ideal buyer.

I include these categories in that definition:

- **Emotion** – Sorrow, joy, vulnerability, fear, courage, etc. I especially like to focus on the eight persuasion desires I listed earlier.
- **Entertainment** – Messages of joy, fun, and distraction.
- **Education** – Secrets to success, strategies, how-to, and skill building.

- **Hope and Trust** – Messages that lift the soul, bring hope for a better life, and increase their faith in humanity, themselves, and others.
- **Connection** – Share stuff about myself with them, tell stories, help them get to know me like best friends do.

As I said, about 80% of your emails should fall within one of these categories.

Salt the Oats

When you write your Value Emails, remember that you're doing all this for two primary purposes:

First, bring value!

You're a Bridge Builder, making the Transformational Journey of your ideal buyer possible, more enjoyable, and easier. Be generous in giving real value.

Second, sell stuff!

Yes, we're in business and that means we need to keep an eye on the profits. As my wife, Margie, says, "Someone has to pay for the party!"

Your value emails need to be purposeful in "salting the oats"… or, in other words, pre-suading them to want to buy from you when you make them an offer.

Rational Transitions

As you will see, the framework includes five Value Emails that lead to Offer Emails that lead to a Deadline Sequence.

The transition from value emails to offer emails needs to be done in rational, logical ways if you want to maintain your ideal buyer's attention.

Imagine you're in a conversation at a dinner party and talking about a recent SCUBA diving trip to the Roatan Barrier Reef.

As you describe the brilliant colors of the reef and the astonishing variety of the sea life, your friend says, "Oh, yeah, I know what you're talking about! That reminds me of how the S&P 500 dropped 9% last week. Let me tell you, that was a blow to my portfolio!" ... and then he proceeds to tell you all about his investments.

Would that feel weird? Out of place? Would you wonder how in the world he made a connection between coral reefs and stocks?

Yes, you would! So would I!

I see companies make this very mistake all the time.

I see a number of emails and then, suddenly, I'm being pitched some off-topic product or service. It feels odd and disjointed. My reaction is to tune it out and ignore it.

In sales and marketing, losing the attention of your ideal buyer is the ultimate crime. Attention is everything, and without it, you have nothing.

Your emails are an ongoing private conversation. As you move from one topic to another, be sure to include rational transitions. This will help you keep their attention.

The Soft Offer

One of the most powerful things you can do is engage your list in a number of micro-commitments.

These are small, simple actions they can take to move them along their journey.

Using a Soft Offer, you invite them to take action or buy something inexpensive from you.

The Soft Offer shows up in the postscript of your emails. You can see examples in the Nurturing Sequence templates and swipe files found in your bonus materials.

If you have—or can create—something that is inexpensive like a cheat sheet, mini-course, resource, or tool, you can offer it to them here.

If you don't have something small to offer them, create a plan to build up a reservoir of things like this. You only need 3-5 because you can repeatedly offer them.

For example, if you run 2-3 Nurturing Sequences a month, you can focus on one Soft Offer in each sequence. That means they would only see the same offer every month or two. If they already have it, they will ignore it or you can get fancy and have the CRM dynamically remove the offer from their emails.

The tone is very much along the lines of, "Hey, I just told you about this cool idea. I thought you might like to get this tool that I use to make it easy to implement. I normally sell this for $99, but you can use this special link to get it right now for just $19. Hope it helps!"

Notice how this isn't a hard sell or push. Just a generous, genuine tip for them, at a huge discount. You can include something like this in just about every email. It will generate you additional revenue, create a pattern of your ideal buyer seeing you be thoughtful and generous, and help them consistently make micro-commitments to you.

The net effect is higher response rates, higher loyalty, and higher engagement... which leads to a better life for your ideal buyer—exactly what you're trying to achieve.

Full Offer Presentation

On Day 6 of this sequence, you present them with your full offer. You have a few ways to do this...

Short Copy – If you have a robust sales letter and/or sales video for your full offer, you can send them a very short email that sounds something like this:

"As promised, I have something very exciting to show you that I think is exactly what you want right now.

Click on this link to get the full details. [LINK]

Remember, I'm only keeping this offer open for 72 hours. Don't miss out! Check it out today!

See it now... [LINK]"

Long Copy – In this approach, your email will be much longer, between 500 and 1500 words.

This is a great place to tell the backstory to your offer, explain the WHY, and let them hear your passion and purpose.

You will still need a sales page and order process, but a longer email allows you to engage with them a little more and tease out the offer a little more.

Which approach is best?

That depends on two factors:

First: Awareness Level. Remember when we talked about this in relation to ads and social media posts?

The same principles apply when presenting your offer in the Nurturing Sequence. Here are the guidelines again:

- Highly aware of their challenge and desire = Short Length Copy
- Highly familiar with you and your solution = Short Length Copy
- Less aware of their challenge and desire = Medium Length Copy
- Less aware of you and your solution = Medium Length Copy
- Unaware of their challenge and desire = Long Length Copy

- Unaware of you and your solution = Long Length Copy

Second: Your Preferred Style. Every email you send both trains your ideal buyer and connects you to them.

I am very comfortable on camera and ad-libbing content.

Others much prefer writing and would be terrified to talk to a camera.

Over time, your list will become accustomed to learning about offers from you on email, on long-copy sales letters, or via video, depending on how you usually communicate with them.

Would you like to read a longer email and have all the details right there? Use that method.

Do you prefer videos or long-copy sales letters? Use those.

Over time, the best strategy is to have all modalities... but right now, you are focused on building out a single funnel and making money as fast as possible! So, pick a method and run with it. They all work.

I once was on my way to the airport and had a brilliant idea for an offer. We got past security and I found a relatively quiet corner. I pulled out my phone and shot a 7:42 video raving about my idea and the offer.

It went out the next day and created a very solid six-figure return for me.

On another promo, I was working with my friend and mentor, RC Peck, selling his investment strategy course. I wrote an email, titled "The Financial Event Your Great - Grandchildren Will Talk About With Awe", with 1,378 words.

That one email performed so well that we were able to skip the sales video and email and go straight to a detailed order page. We tested this with almost a dozen joint-venture partners in the financial newsletter community and it performed equally well across the board. Open rates were over 30% and conversion rates were as high as 51% among readers.

My point is this... pick a style. They all work.

Later in this chapter, we'll talk about all the elements you need to make the Nurturing Sequence work, including Core Offer, sales letter, video, order form, etc.

72-Hour Deadline Sequence

Deadlines create urgency. Urgency, especially the fear of missing out (sometimes referred to as FOMO), is a very powerful selling emotion.

Remember Sir Isaac Newton's first law of physics?

> A body at rest will remain at rest unless an outside force acts on it, and a body in motion at a constant velocity will remain in motion in a straight line unless acted upon by an outside force.

Read that law again carefully because it applies to human behavior as well.

Your ideal buyer is already living.

Every second of every minute of every hour of every day is already filled up with something. They are eating, sleeping, going to work, brushing their teeth, going on vacation, spending time with friends and family, etc.

With rare exception, not one of them has a spot on their calendar that says they should spend money on your stuff.

They are like a body at rest... or a body in motion... and they will stay that way until an outside force acts on them.

That outside force is you, specifically you imposing a real deadline on them. This deadline demands a decision from them—Yes or No.

You will create a 72-hour deadline sequence. This gives them three full days to consider the offer and make a decision that they will not regret later.

This point about them not regretting their decision later is very important. Each interaction with you should be something that they are sure about, happy about, and can brag to others about.

The long-term relationship with your ideal buyer is MUCH more important than any one sale or purchase. As you build out your campaigns, keep that truth in mind. First and foremost, nurture the relationship with them by helping them along their journey.

The 72-Hour Deadline Sequence begins casually enough. You lay out the offer and tell them they have three days to decide.

The closer you get to the deadline, the more urgent your messages will become.

And, of course, if they buy at any point, you remove them from the deadline sequence to preserve their trust and confidence in you.

Up to Two Emails Per Day, Three Days in a Row

After you activate the 72-Hour Deadline, you will send up to two emails per day for those three days.

Here is how that works:

- **Day 7, Morning Email, 7 am**
    - Send the first email to everyone on your list, except anyone that already owns the offer.
- **Day 7, Evening Email, 7 pm**
    - Send the second email at 7 pm to everyone on your list that has not yet *opened* the morning email.
    - If they open the morning email, DO NOT send the evening email to them. Your CRM can track this for you.
    - If they purchase the offer, remove them from the sequence immediately.
- **Day 8, Morning Email, 7 am**

- Send this email to everyone on your list that has not yet purchased.
- **Day 8, Evening Email, 7 pm**
  - Send to everyone who did NOT *open* the Day 8 Morning Email.
  - Do not send to offer owners.
- **Day 9, Morning Email, 7 am**
  - Send to everyone who has not purchased the offer yet.
- **Day 9, Evening Email, 7 pm**
  - Send to everyone that did not **click** on the order link in the email.
  - Do not send to offer owners.

Notice that the first two days, the evening email gets sent to anyone who does not open the morning email.

On the third day, you will send the final reminder to everyone who did not click on the order link inside the email.

This pattern shows a great deal of respect for your ideal buyer. It builds their trust and confidence in you. Sending too many emails will fatigue and irritate your list.

The Nurturing Sequence Framework

With these key ideas and definitions in mind, here is the actual framework with a brief insight and instructions on each email:

Volume and Timing

You will send out a maximum of 12 emails over a nine-day period.

There is a lot of discussion about what time of day and day of the week you should send your emails. The reality is this... if you are an important part of their life, it really doesn't matter. They will find your emails and pay attention to them.

Additionally, the Nurturing Sequence is triggered automatically when they finalize their initial purchase sequence, so there isn't really a way to control which day of the week it begins. Your ideal buyers will all be on different, personalized schedules based on when they enter your funnel.

It is important to set the time of day because toward the end of the Nurturing Sequence, you will send up to two emails—one in the morning and one in the evening. Because of this, I set all of my emails to be sent at 7 am and 7 pm. Your CRM will automatically adjust for time zone differences so that everyone will get it at their 7 am and 7 pm.

Schedule Details

Here are the exact details of the schedule with some pro-tips included...

- **Email #1 – Send Day 1, 7 am: Value**
  - Emotion-Based. Use this email to emotionally connect. Tell a story. Be vulnerable. Be sincere and genuine. Motivate and inspire them.
  - Soft Offer: In the PS, invite them to take simple, specific action and comment on their experience on social media or email.
- **Email #2 – Send Day 2, 7 am: Value**
  - Education-Based. Give them a viable, simple, quick-win powerful secret.
  - Soft Offer: Low-priced offer or specific call to action, as outlined above.
- **Email #3 – Send Day 3, 7 am: Value**

- Entertainment-Based. Spend time in this email simply entertaining and connecting with them. For example, you can tell a simple story that inspires them and illustrates a point.
- Soft Offer: Can be the same offer from Email #2. Keep it very short and simple in the PS.

• **Day 4 – Email #4 – Send Day 4, 7 am: Value**
  - Hope and Trust Focus. Identify a serious problem or top desire you know they have. Give some examples of people that have solved the issue or fulfilled the desire. You are "salting the oats" for your offer. Include proof that you're a master at overcoming this problem to increase trust and build hope in them.
  - Soft Offer: Can be the same offer from Email #2. Keep it very short and simple in the PS. You can copy and paste so that it is exactly the same or change a few words.

• **Day 5 – Email #5 – Send Day 5, 7 am: Value + Offer and Deadline Teaser**
  - Education Focus. Continue talking about the desire or challenge you identified in Email #4. Then provide them a solution. Tell them HOW to solve it, not specifically WHAT to do. You can also give them a quick-win idea that helps them solve a tiny aspect of the challenge or gives them a taste of enjoying their top desire.
  - Offer & Deadline Teaser. Tell them that tomorrow you have something exciting for them that will be a guaranteed, 100% solution to their challenge or fulfillment of their desire. Tell them you're offering it on a limited basis and they will only have 72 hours to take advantage of the offer. You're setting them up for the full offer and deadline announcement on Day 6.

• **Day 6 – Email #6 – Send Day 6, 7 am: Full Offer Details + Deadline Starts**

- Full Offer Focus. Present the full offer using your method of choice, i.e.... long or short copy email.
- Announce the Deadline. The 72 hours officially starts the following morning.
- Call to Action: Offer Open Now! Tell them they can get an early jump on the offer and buy now. Include 3-5 order page links throughout the email.

- **Day 7 – Email #7, Send Day 7, 7 am: Offer Social Proof + Deadline Reminder**
    - Social Proof Focus. The bulk of this email should be social proof. Quotes, case studies, comments from social media, etc. I like to simply say, "Here's what others have said about this offer..." You can use 3-10 points, depending on how long they are.
    - Offer Summary. Outline the offer details again.
    - Call to Action. Provide 3-4 links throughout the email directing them to the sales page.
    - Deadline Reminder. At the top of the email and again at the bottom, have a reminder of the deadline. The one at the top can be Eyebrow Copy, stating the offer ends in three days. At the bottom of the email, after the signature line and postscript, include an actual countdown timer that is ticking away, reminding them that time is running out. Include a note in the call to action as well.

- **Day 7 – Email #8 – Send Day 7, 7 pm: Did you see this?**
    - Did you see? I like to put a short note saying, "Hey, Bob—Did you see the email I sent this morning? It is really important. Here it is again, just in case you missed it..." Then copy and paste your Day 7 Morning Email.
    - Remember, only send to people who did NOT open the morning email. If they did open it, you can assume they saw it and not bug them again with it.

- **Day 8 – Email #9 – Send Day 8, 7 am: Value + Deadline Reminder**
  - Education Focus. Send them a surprise secret. Think of this as a preview of the offer you're making them. Tell them how to do something, give them the inside story, or reveal a juicy secret. Show them that even if they don't buy this offer, you are 100% committed to helping them along their transformation journey. Ask yourself, "If this is the last email I ever send them, what can I tell them that would be super valuable to them and help them?"
  - Offer Summary. Review the offer and its key benefits.
  - Call to Action. Include 3-4 links and calls to action, including:
  - Deadline Reminder. Include the countdown timer at the top and bottom of the email. Remind them in the copy.
  - Scarcity Notice: Include any other elements of scarcity you have, such as limited quantity, etc.
- **Day 8 – Email #10 – Send Day 8, 7 pm, Non-Opens: Offer Details + 24-hour Deadline Reminder**
  - Deadline Reminder – They are about 24 hours away from the offer ending. Put that in the subject line. Include ticking timer in the header and footer of the email. Include reminders in the copy.
  - Summary of the Details and Benefits. You can copy and paste bullet points or details you've sent them before.
  - Call to Action. 3-4 links to the sales page.
  - Only send to people who did not open the Day 8 morning email.
- **Day 9 – Email #11 – Send Day 9, 7 am, Non-Opens: Ends Today, Proof Elements, Offer Details**
  - Deadline Focus. Begin with a subject line and opening sentence notifying them that it is the last day. They need to act now!
  - Social and Factual Proof. Use the previous testimonials/social proof or include new ones if you have them. Include more

factual proof points like a scientific study, historical proof, independent analysis, or studies, etc. At this point in the sequence, you have given them a great deal of emotion and stories and they might just need factual talking points to convince themselves (and their spouse!) that spending the money is a great move.
- Summary of Offer Details. Include the summary... again!
- Call to Action. Include the call to action and links in 3-4 different ways and places in the email.

- **Day 9 – Email #12 – Send Day 9, 7 pm, Non-Clicks – Last Call, Offer Summary, Direct Plea**
  - Deadline Reminder: Ticking countdown timer at the top and bottom.
  - Last Call! This email should be very short. Be direct.
  - Offer and Benefit Summary. You can change it up if you want, but you don't need to. Copy and paste.
  - Direct Plea – Imagine if you were sitting down with your best friend. They had been sick and you found something that would be a 100% cure for them. They are not sure about it. How would you talk to them? How would you plead for them to take it and be healed? How much love and passion and concern would you put into that argument? That is what this email is all about. Get super real with them. Be passionate. Be loving. Be bold.
  - Call to Action. Links, closing statements, etc. Get them to go!

The Steps to Create Your Flagship Offer and Sell It With The Nurturing Sequence

1 – Define the Deliverable

As with everything, before you create your Flagship Offer, you need to define what you're offering them.

What is the next step in their journey and how can you build a bridge for them? At this stage of the game, you want to offer them your "Flagship Offer".

The Flagship Offer should be a comprehensive solution to their challenges or way to fulfill their desires. Whereas other offers to this point have been about taking slices or putting a microscope to a section of their journey, this should be about the whole journey... at least a bite-sized piece of it.

For example, this book is a comprehensive guide to building your first funnel. A funnel is manageable. You can do it in a few weeks and start making money.

I really help people in every aspect of their business and personal Transformational Journey... but there is no way to write a book or build a course that addresses everything from thinking of an idea to creating holding companies.

But, a funnel is central to every aspect of business success. By outlining the details of a proven, successful funnel, I'm giving you a tool to transform your business, your income, and your lifestyle.

You can think of your Flagship Offer in the same way. What is a comprehensive deliverable you can make good on in a relatively short period of time? What process will be transformational for them?

2 – Choose the Format

Your Flagship Offer will be one of the formats I outlined in previous chapters. Any of them will work. Pick one and go!

3 – Create Your Flagship Offer

Again, you will follow the same creative process we used to create your other offers. You should be a pro at it now. You can use the checklist I created for you.

4 – Format and Shine It Up

Once you write, record the video, and create your resources and tools, clean it up.

How things look is really important, as I've mentioned before. One more quick story…

In 2003, we lived in Helena, MT. I owned a fundraising company that specialized in working with pro-family, humanitarian organizations like Boy Scouts, Easter Seals, Catholic Relief Services, Right to Life, etc.

Business was going very well and I wanted to move into a new home to fit our growing family (we only had five children at the time with number six on the way).

Helena has a beautiful "Mansion District" with a few dozen gorgeous mansions dating back to the gold rush days. We looked at one that was for rent.

It was perfect! In talking to the management company, they said I'd qualify, no problem, and they would get things arranged in the next few days.

A week went by and no word. Then two weeks. Finally, I called.

"This is Joshua Boswell. I'm calling about my lease application. What's the status?"

"Yes, Mr. Boswell," the man said in a rather snooty and belittling voice. "We declined your application and are returning your deposit."

I was shocked.

"Ok. Can you tell me why?"

"We looked at your company website and it showed up as 'under construction'. The managers all agreed that there is no way you could be making this kind of money from a company that can't even put up a website. We don't believe you're legit."

"What?! But I don't even use my website to make sales or run my business. You need to reconsider this. How do I appeal?"

"You can't. Look, Mr. Boswell, I'm very busy and don't have time to argue with liars and cons."

And with that, he hung up.

No matter how I disliked it, they 100% judged me by my "cover". Sadly, your ideal buyer will do the same with you.

Again, you do not need to make it perfect, but it does need to be professional and appeal to the level of your ideal buyer.

5 – Write the Sales Copy and Video Script

Using the templates provided in this book and in the bonus materials, write the sales letter and video script.

> Pro-Tip: If you have the money to hire a professional copywriter, this is one place where it could be an EXCELLENT investment for you. If you want to go that route, I have access to thousands of professionally trained persuasive writers. Just contact us and we can help you find the right writer for your needs. copywriter@strahes.com or www.Strahes.com/copywriter.

If you do it yourself, be sure to have it reviewed as we discussed earlier.

6 – Set Up Your Offer in the CRM

Create the offer in the CRM. Set up automations to have it added to the buyer's library when they purchase.

7 – Create the Order Page

Write the copy for the order page. Set it up inside your CRM.

8 – Create the "Thank You" Page

This "Thank You" Page will follow the same patterns as the final "Thank You" Page in your initial funnel sequence.

It should have a sincere "thank you" message, plus provide them with a way to go deeper into your world.

9 – Write the Welcome and Deliverables Emails

Like with the other offers, when someone buys, you need to instantly communicate to them about how to access their purchase.

Also, especially with the Flagship Offer, it is very important to include an email series that helps them consume this offer.

Conclusion and Summary

Let's go back to where we started… I was talking to Bernie and suggested they needed a Nurturing Sequence to improve sales and make their global launches a smashing success…

Because we were dealing with millions of email addresses, both buyers and subscribers, we took their list and heavily segmented it.

This means we analyzed it for different psychographic and demographic groups. We ended up with over 67 different target groups. Each group had its own set of benefits, keywords, and stories.

Remember, the best sales and marketing is a one-on-one, private conversation with another human being.

I wrote a Nurturing Sequence for them that became the foundation. Then, we had their in-house marketing team customize the sequence so that it was appropriate for each of the 67 segments.

Then, we hit send!

The results?

Some of the segments had open rates of over 70% (that's really good, by the way!). The total conversion rate across the board, on all email segments, was over 23%... and brought in just over $24.1 million.

I'm not promising you those kinds of returns, but I can promise that using a Nurturing Sequence as I've outlined it will increase your sales.

It is 12 emails... 12 emails that are vital to your profits, your success, and your growth.

Make this a top priority and enjoy the rewards!

Action Checklist

- [ ] **1 - Define the Deliverable** - What is the next step in their journey and how can you build a bridge for them? At this stage of the game, you want to offer them your "Flagship Offer"
What is a comprehensive deliverable you can make good on in a relatively short period of time? What process will be transformational for them?

- [ ] **2 - Choose the Format** - Your Flagship Offer will be one of the formats I outlined in previous chapters. Any of them will work. Pick one and go!

- [ ] **3 - Create Your Flagship Offer** - You should be a pro at this by now. You can use the checklist I created for you in your bonus materials.

THE BRIDGE BUILDER METHOD

- ☐ **4 - Format and Shine it Up** - Once you write, record the video, and create your resources and tools, clean it up. How things look is really important, as I've mentioned before.

- ☐ **5 - Write the Sales Copy and Video Script** - Create the offer in the CRM. Set up automations to have it added to the buyer's library when they purchase.

- ☐ **6 - Set up Your Offer in the CRM** - Create the offer in the CRM. Set up automations to have it added to the buyer's library when they purchase.

- ☐ **7 - Create the Order Page** - Write the copy for the order page. Set it up inside your CRM.

- ☐ **8 - Create the Thank You Page** This "Thank You" Page will follow the same patterns as the final "Thank You" Page in your initial funnel sequence.

- ☐ **9 - Write the Welcome and Deliverables Emails** - Like with the other offers, when someone buys, you need to instantly communicate to them about how to access their purchase.

  Also, especially with the Flagship Offer, it is very important to include an email series that helps them consume this offer.

CONCLUSION

The "Bridge" That Saved a Life

Quin was a brilliant boy with blazing red hair, one of those kids who's always throwing baseballs through windows and dousing cats in kerosene.

When he was six, a counselor in public school doped him up with Ritalin to break his spirits and "keep order in the classroom".

His parents pulled him out and placed him in private school. Quin's new teachers 'got' him. They channeled his energy and helped him express his creative genius. He thrived under their mentorship.

In 2004, Margie had just given birth to our sixth child, Brigham, just a few weeks before our oldest child, Esther, turned seven years old. We homeschool our children. Teaching, nursing an infant, monitoring the diaper status of the three youngest, making meals, etc. It was just a crazy time for us.

Margie was tired and needed a break. To help relieve the pressure, we found the same Christian private school that Quin's parents found and enrolled the children.

Shortly after the school year started, the school's director, Susan, invited me to be on the Board of Directors. During our first board meeting, I discovered something was terribly wrong. The global financial crisis had not been kind to private schools. Enrollment had dropped sharply, leaving them grasping for money.

"I'm afraid if something doesn't change in the next few months, we'll have to close up before next semester," Susan said.

"Wait a minute," I said. "I just moved my family from Montana to have them attend this school. We've only been here a few months and you're telling me the school is going to close? That is crazy!"

Susan stirred uncomfortably in her seat. I could see she was extremely stressed and under massive pressure.

"I'm afraid it's true. I thought enrollment would be higher and we'd have the funds we need. But we don't."

I sat for a minute thinking. If something didn't change, the school would close, forcing Quin to go back into public school, where he would return to being a misfit instead of a genius. My children would return home, putting huge pressure back on Margie.

None of that was acceptable to me.

"Ok, Susan, here's the deal. I'm going to fix this for you, but you need to let me have full access to the other board members and the parents. Plus, you need to trust me, no matter how uncomfortable you might feel during the process. Deal?"

She very slowly nodded her head.

"The first thing we are going to do is get some immediate cash in so I can run a targeted direct-response campaign to the community. How much cash on hand do we have to work with right now?"

"Only enough for three months of payroll. The landlord for this building is deferring rent. That's all we have."

CONCLUSION

"Ok, I have another plan..."

I got on the phone and personally called the top 10 wealthiest families in the school. Each was invited to a special five-course meal catered by a gourmet chef. At the end of dinner, I made a presentation and outlined the school's dire situation.

"Here's the deal. We need $15,000 to run a marketing campaign to fill up enrollment before next semester and sustain it for next year. No one leaves until I have the full amount."

Before the night was over, the school had $15,000 in hand, with a pledge for twice that if needed.

It wasn't needed. We only spent $5,000 and they kept the rest for immediate expenses.

I built the campaign using the bridge building secrets outlined in this book. Within a week of launching the campaign, enrollment doubled. Every class was filled up by the end of the semester, so a large waiting list was created. Almost overnight, it became an elite status to be part of that school. This effectively ensured enrollment for the next few years would be just fine.

My children became best friends with Quin. The school was amazing for all of them.

As beautiful as that was, little did I know how crucial saving the school would be to Quin and his family.

Five months later, en route to a business meeting, Quin's dad's private plane was struck by lightning and crashed into a lake. All four passengers were instantly killed.

Quin's mom was pregnant with their fifth child at the time. Her world blew apart, threatening to destroy Quin and his siblings as well. In those dark hours, it was the staff and other parents from the private school that rallied around Quin's family. We became her support, love, rock, and strength.

Moms and dads organized to provide meals, rides to school, activities, counseling, and tutoring for Quin and his siblings.

I and others reached out to Quin and his brothers and sisters. While we could never take their father's place, we took them under our wing.

Today, Quin has grown into a respectful, well-rounded, responsible, enterprising young man. In part, he is what he is today because, in a crisis, his schoolmates and their parents rallied around him. Those people would not have been there for Quinn had the school shut its doors.

I witnessed a miracle that year. It was a miracle that would not or could not have happened if Quin had been just another ADHD kid sentenced to a state-run educational prison with 500 other edu-clones.

Bridge Building —the process of meeting a total stranger online, and turning them into a best friend that is loyal to you and buys repeatedly from you— is magical. It has the power to transform your life and bless the lives of your ideal buyers.

Now is the time to go to work. Follow this outline. Don't worry about all the things you COULD do... stay focused on doing what you SHOULD do, right now, to build bridges for your ideal buyer and grow your business.

I believe that, whatever your business is, if you are honestly seeking to bring value to others, to help them in their journey, you will transform lives... your ideal buyers and yours.

ACKNOWLEDGEMENTS

Acknowledgements

No man is an island. I am no exception. My life is not my own. It is a compilation of the love, kindness, teachings and corrections by dozens of people. In naming them, I will miss some, but that omission will be totally unintentional and due more to my imperfections and the limited space in this book than to any imagined ingratitude.

First and foremost, God has been incredibly gracious with me. He has moved me around, connected me with people, inspired ideas, and blessed me in countless ways. Second, I am unspeakably grateful to my dear wife Margie. She is the mother of our eleven children. She is patient and powerful. Kind and persistent. Beautiful and fierce. She is my best friend and has, in every sense possible, been God's hands in fashioning and framing my life. Third, I'm incredibly grateful to my children. In particular, Joshua, Jared and Isaac. These boys started doing business projects with me in their early teens and have been the best business partners a man could ever wish for. They are incredible humans and amazing entrepreneurs. Fourth, when I was a teenager, my mother, Kristine, fought like crazy to raise six children on her own. She found ways to stay at home with us and still make money. It was she that gave me the passion for family, financial freedom, and business. I miss you, Mom.

In my professional life, I have gleaned volumes of wisdom from a number of key people in my life. The ideas, strategies and secrets in this book can easily be traced back to these people and their personal coaching and mentoring, including: Perry Marshall, Bob Bly, Katie Yeakle, Rebecca Matter, Mark Ford, Brendon Burchard, Rick Sapio, Richard Koch and Clayton Makepeace who left us way too early.

Finally, when I was a young boy and my parents divorced, my 5th grade teacher, Miss Ann Mitchell (the Left-Handed Genius!) gave me love and a love of learning. Mr. John Pool, my 6th grade teacher, taught me how to research and think logically. Susan Winn, my high school English teacher that put up with me for three years, infused a passion for writing and communication.

I express my love and deep appreciation for all of you. Not only did you make this book possible, you made me possible.

About Joshua T. Boswell

Looking through the windshield of the Chrysler LaBaron station wagon, my 11 year old mind was screaming, "I just want my daddy! Daddy come back!" But he didn't come back - at least not then.

Dad walked down the road and disappeared from my sight... and my life for the next five years. Mom filled the void as best she could, financially, emotionally and spiritually. But still, nothing fully replaces the influence of a daddy. Those years infused in my soul three passions:

- A passion for God - He was and is my strength.
- A passion for family - I wanted to be a daddy more than anything.
- And a passion for wealth - time and money to live life on my own terms.

My wife, Margie and I met on a Friday night, got engaged the following Tuesday and then were married in 2.5 months. As of this writing we have been married for over 27 years. We are the proud parents of eleven children, with spouses and grandchildren adding to the joy every year.

The first 10 years of marriage had me fully enrolled in the business school of hard knocks. I started a number of businesses... Some succeeded, others did less than grand. But I learned from all of them. My clients gave me a wonderful opportunity to see inside some of the most successful businesses and non-profit organizations in the world.

I spent more than 12 years as a freelance copywriter and marketing consultant. I began teaching other writers and entrepreneurs. Today, more than 35,000 freelancers and business owners have taken my courses and participated in my training. Thousands have been able to

ABOUT JOSHUA T. BOSWELL

transform their lives, achieve their financial goals and have success in life.

My clients include Corel, Sony, Toshiba, Google, General Motors, Agora, AWAI, Perry Marshall and Associates, Easter Seals-Goodwill, The Boy Scouts of America, Right to Life, Christian Children's Fund, Catholic Relief Services and dozens of others.

All of my business ventures have one thing in common: Your growth. I believe that honest capitalists and entrepreneurs do more good for the world than just about anything else. My mission is to help you grow your business, grow your wealth and grow yourself. To get to know me more and see how we can win together, visit me at: www.Strahes.com or www.JoshuaBoswell.com